D0618013

PARANORMAL FILES

ATLANTIS
AND OTHER
LOST WORLDS

Stuart Webb

ROSEN
PUBLISHING®

New York

This edition published in 2013 by:

The Rosen Publishing Group, Inc.
29 East 21st Street, New York, NY 10010

Editor and Picture Researcher: Joe Harris
U.S. Editor: Kathy Campbell
Design: Jane Hawkins
Cover Design: Jane Hawkins

Library of Congress Cataloging-in-Publication Data

Webb, Stuart.
Atlantis and other lost worlds/Stuart Webb.
     p. cm.—(Paranormal files)
Includes bibliographical references and index.
ISBN 978-1-4488-7173-5 (library binding)
1. Atlantis (Legendary place) 2. Lemuria. 3. Lost continents. I. Title.
GN751.W37 2013
398.23'4—dc23

2011043004

Manufactured in China

SL002143US

Picture Credits:
Cover: Shutterstock.
Interior: Bill Stoneham: 23, 24, 58. Corbis: 5, 15, 31, 43, 46. Frank Joseph: 11, 13, 35, 36, 51, 53, 57.
Shutterstock: 1, 6, 9, 17, 18, 20, 27, 29, 33, 38, 40, 45, 48, 55, 61, 62, 64, 67, 68, 70, 72, 75, 80.

CPSIA Compliance Information: Batch #S12YA: For further information, contact Rosen Publishing, New York, New York, at 1-800-237-9932.

CONTENTS

THE LEGEND OF ATLANTIS AND LEMURIA

Atlantis is a legendary city on an island in the Atlantic Ocean, first described by the ancient Greek philosopher Plato, who lived between 492 and 347 BCE. In his dialogues, Plato describes Atlantis as an oceanic empire, based on the island of Atlas, which lay "beyond the Pillars of Heracles" (the Straits of Gibraltar).

A Global Power

According to those people who believe in its reality, Atlantis existed in about 9,000 BCE (or the 1200s BCE according to another interpretation). Its empire allegedly stretched from the North American copper mines of Michigan's Upper Peninsula, the shores of Mexico and Colombia in the west, to Italy and Egypt in the east, encompassing more territories and peoples than even the Roman Empire at its height. But, says Plato, in the middle of Atlantis's war against the Mediterranean world, the island of Atlas, of which Atlantis was the capital, sank "in a single day and night" of earthquakes and floods.

The Island and Its City

According to legend, the island of Atlas – named after a mythical Titan who supported the sky – was mountainous and broadly forested. South of its towering, dormant volcano was a plain 34 miles (55 kilometers) long by 23 miles (37 km) wide. It was irrigated by a network of canals carrying water to the crops flourishing in the richly fertile volcanic soil.

South of this agricultural complex lay the city of Atlantis, capital of the oceanic empire. Plato records that the metropolis was made up of alternating circles of land and water, interconnected by bridged canals accommodating both ship and foot traffic. Each of these artificial islands was surrounded by high walls interspersed with mighty watchtowers manned by soldiers. The smallest, central island bore the imperial residence and the magnificent Temple of Poseidon. A horse racetrack occupied the city's outermost land ring.

A visitor at that time, says Plato, would have been awed by the city's walls, not only for their enormous dimensions, but also for the sheets of orichalcum (high-grade copper) and mosaics of

judgment of the other rulers on any complaint made against them, as demanded by the laws of Poseidon. The laws also prevented the kings from making war on each other and required them to take united action against any external enemy.

semi-precious minerals gleaming in the sunlight. The Temple of Poseidon was dominated, it is said, by a colossal statue of the sea god in his chariot, pulled by winged horses.

Volcanic rock, being so abundant, was the main building material, and resulted in the black (lava), white (pumice) and red (tufa) colors Plato said characterized Atlantean architecture, supplemented by decorative sheets of orichalcum.

Rulers of Atlantis

Plato explains that the empire was governed by ten kings, all directly descended from the sea-god founder of their civilization. The kings had absolute power over their own cities and regions, but submitted to the

LOST WORLD FILES

DID ATLANTIS EXIST?

The legend of Atlantis has been a source of fascination ever since it was rediscovered by scholars in the 17th century. But is there any truth to it? Atlantologists (seekers of Atlantis) speculate that a large landmass may once have existed in the location of the Mid-Atlantic Ridge. Geologists say that, if so, it would have been wracked by volcanoes and earthquakes, so it would have been an unlikely homeland for a successful civilization. Most Plato scholars believe that his Atlantis was imaginary, or perhaps based on the island of Santorini in the Mediterranean, which was devastated by an eruption in about 1600 BCE. The arguments continue, and will probably only be settled when technological advances permit a systematic survey of the ocean floor.

The head of the House of Atlas acted as emperor, whose decisions took precedent and were final. The laws of Poseidon encouraged the kings to rule with wisdom and restraint. Any who deviated from the laws were liable to charges of holy perjury and oath-breaking, offenses that were subject to harsh punishments.

A Military Power

Legend tells us that at its height, Atlantis boasted immense armed forces to protect its far-flung empire. According to Plato, the Atlanteans fielded no fewer than 79,600 men-at-arms. These included 7,200 hoplites (heavily armed foot soldiers) and the same number of archers, supported by an additional 33,600 slingers and javelin-throwers. They were joined by 10,000 chariots, each one manned by a driver and warrior bearing a light shield. Atlantis was primarily a sea power. Her 14,400 naval personnel – marines, sailors, shipwrights and dock hands – serviced 1,200 ships, which would have made it by far the biggest fleet of the ancient world.

Lemuria

Lemuria, or Mu, is the name of a mythical lost land said to have existed long ago in the Indian and/or Pacific Oceans. In 1864, zoologist Philip Sclater

Plato claimed that the citizens of Atlantis worshipped the sea god Poseidon.

pointed out that fossils of lemurs and other related primates were found on Madagascar (an island off Africa) as well as in India. He proposed that both countries had once been part of a larger continent, which he named Lemuria (after "lemur"). Sclater's theory attracted support from some scientists, some of whom suggested that Lemuria had extended across parts of the Pacific Ocean as well.

Pacific Culture

The lost continent of Lemuria became a popular idea among 19th-century occultists such as Helena Blavatsky, William Scott-Elliot and James Bramwell. According to their theories, Mu was a culture that spread its influence over many Pacific islands before they were swallowed up by the ocean. Forced to abandon their homes, the Lemurians dispersed, settling in Melanesia and Polynesia. Some moved to the Americas, influencing the early cultures there. By studying and comparing modern-day Pacific cultures, the occultists tried to construct a picture of what they believed to be a single root culture: Lemuria.

The occultists theorized that Mu existed at the same time as Atlantis, but the two civilizations were very different. While Atlantis was a technologically advanced, imperialist culture, the Lemurians were a simple, devout, seafaring people whose chief purpose in sailing to other parts of the world was to spread their spiritual beliefs.

Architecture

The Lemurians built ceremonial centers, sacred sculptures and roads, but no cities. The evidence for this, according to the occultists, lay in Mu's influence on later cultures – for example, the roads in Micronesia's Tonga and Malden Island, the monumental sculpted heads of Mexico's Olmecs, the colossi of Easter Island and the ancient city at Nan Madol in the Caroline Islands. Based on this evidence, the occultists believe that Lemurian building styles were largely right-angled and rectangular, contrasting with Atlantean architecture, which was predominantly curved and circular.

LOST WORLD FILES

DID LEMURIA EXIST?

The scientific community no longer believes that Lemuria existed – at least not in the Indian Ocean. According to the theory of plate tectonics, accepted now by all geologists, Madagascar and India were indeed once part of the same landmass, but plate movement caused India to break away millions of years ago and move to its present location. The original landmass broke apart – it did not sink beneath the sea.

Culture and Society

The occultists have tried to reconstruct what Lemurian culture and society might have been like. The Lemurians apparently lived in small villages of wood-and-grass homes, clustered around their great stone ceremonial centers and usually located by the sea or a river. The ceremonial centers were the focal points of Lemurian society. They comprised plazas surrounded by broad staircases leading up to spacious platforms, surmounted by smaller temples.

Political authority in Lemuria, they say, rested with a single spiritual leader who was regarded with awe by the whole population as a living god. He ruled with the help of a hierarchy of priests, who ruled as much through spiritual example as through law.

Crime was apparently rare in Lemuria, and there were no prisons, capital punishment or police. A small number of part-time guards answered only to the spiritual leader and his priestly colleagues, who acted as judges when occasion demanded. Thieves and liars were subjected to extra religious training. More serious cases, including repeat offenders, violent troublemakers or murderers, were banished to distant, wilder lands.

Music, Art and Language

According to believers in Lemuria, the Lemurians were a musically skilled

Seeker's Account

A SPIRITUAL PEOPLE

The occultist W.S. Cerve wrote of the Lemurians:

"To them the spiritual part of the world was the most important, because it was the only real aspect and only dependable and safe side of life. Thousands of years of accumulated knowledge had taught them that the very foundation upon which they stood, composed as it was of earthly materials, and subject to the mighty changes that had taken place and would take place, was a most unreliable and unreal part of life."

people, excelling in the performance of a cappella singing, yet another legacy preserved among the Polynesians. They created colored sand-paintings, an art that spread with their migrations to the American Southwest, among the Navaho Indians, and, in the opposite direction, to Tibet. The Lemurian word for art, "ord," according to W.S. Cerve, "was used only in reference to the Deity."

According to the occultists, the Lemurians invented mathematical computation and accounting in the form of colored knotted cords, a method left behind in both Polynesia and Bolivia. They also developed their own written language and, it is claimed, carried it with them as they traveled east and west, where it became, respectively, the Indus Valley script at Mohenjo Daro, India's first civilization, and the *rongorongo* script of Easter Island. The occultists attest that the similarity between these two distantly separated languages can only be explained by the fact that they are descended from a single ancestral language, developed by the Lemurians.

Contact Between Atlantis and Mu

The Lemurians and Atlanteans were aware of each other, but contact between the two cultures was limited, according to the occultists. The Lemurians did not generally welcome foreigners. Select individuals were allowed temporary stay in Mu for religious training, diplomatic reasons or other sanctioned business. Perhaps the Lemurians' coolness toward visitors from Atlantis stemmed from a nervous mix of disdain and fear. According to Cerve, the Atlanteans referred to them as the "Holy Lemurians" for their religious zeal, or "the blind race," because of the many who apparently suffered eye disorders in Mu. As Atlantis grew increasingly decadent, however, the Atlanteans began to look down on the Lemurians as superstitious and backward.

According to some, the statues of Easter Island are evidence of the existence of Lemuria.

SEEKERS OF ATLANTIS

The earliest known person to describe Atlantis was the Greek philosopher Plato. His narrative concerning Atlantis is contained in two dialogues, the *Timaeus* and the *Kritias*. In the *Timaeus*, Solon, the great Athenian lawgiver, visits Egypt. There, he is told that long ago the Athenians saved Greece and Egypt from invading Atlantean forces. He learned that the kingdom of Atlantis, located on a large island "beyond the Pillars of Heracles," was greater than Libya and Asia Minor combined, exercising dominion over all neighboring islands and the "opposite continent." But in the midst of its war against the Mediterranean world, the island of Atlantis sank "in a single day and night" of earthquakes and floods. In the *Kritias*, Plato describes the geography and society of Atlantis in great detail (see pages 4–6 for a summary of this).

Plato's story of the legendary empire was dismissed as a pagan fiction until it was revived in the 17th century by the German Jesuit priest Athanasius Kircher (1602–80). Kircher was the first scholar to seriously investigate the Atlantis legend. Initially skeptical, he began to reconsider the possibility of such an empire when he noticed similarities in the mythic traditions of numerous cultures in different parts of the world, such as the myth of the Great Flood.

Kircher's Map

Kircher's research led him to an immense collection of source materials at the Vatican Library. It was here that he discovered a single piece of

Seeker's Account
A GREAT TRUTH

Recalling his discovery of common themes in different mythologies, Kircher wrote:

"I confess for a long time I had regarded all this as pure fables to the day when, better instructed in Oriental languages, I judged that all these legends must be, after all, only the development of a great truth."

evidence that made him believe that the legend was based on fact. Among the relatively few surviving documents from imperial Rome, Kircher found a well-preserved treated-leather map purporting to show the configuration and location of Atlantis. The map was not Roman, but brought in the first century CE to Italy from Egypt, where it had been made long before. Kircher copied it precisely, adding only a visual reference to the New World, and published it in his book *Mundus Subterraneus* (The Subterranean World) in 1665.

In the book, Kircher's caption to the map describes it as "a map of the island of Atlantis originally made in Egypt after Plato's description," which suggests it was created some time after the fourth century BCE, perhaps by a Greek mapmaker attached to the Ptolemies – Greeks descended from Alexander the Great and rulers of the Nile Valley from 300 to 30 BCE. It is likely that the map's first home was the Great Library of Alexandria, the foremost repository of knowledge in the ancient world, which was burned down in 392 CE on the orders of the Roman Emperor Theodosius I. If the map had been at Alexandria, it must have been relocated to Rome before the library's

This map of Atlantis was found in the Vatican Library by Athanasius Kircher. Does it show a real place?

destruction. Although the original map vanished some time after 1680, Kircher's version survives to this day.

Kircher's map depicts Atlantis as a large island. It indicates a high, centrally located volcano, most likely meant to represent Mount Atlas, together with six major rivers. Plato's *Kritias* also describes important rivers on the island. That Kircher's map shows six of them perhaps recalls the sacred number of Atlantis – six.

Curiously, the map is depicted with south at the top, contrary to maps in both Kircher's day and ours. This apparent anomaly may be because Egyptian cartographers, even as late as Ptolemaic times, designed their maps with the Upper Nile Valley located in the south ("Upper" refers to its higher elevation), at the top because the river's headwaters are located in the Sudan.

Rudbeck

Olaus Rudbeck (1630–1702) was a Swedish contemporary of Kircher. Professor of Medicine, inventor, designer, astronomer, architect, musician and historian, Rudbeck turned his formidable energy and skills toward a study of the legendary island empire.

After a long period of investigation, he concluded that Atlantis was fact, not fiction, and the greatest civilization in prehistory. From 1679 until his death in 1702, he devoted himself to the writing of *Atlantica*. In this four-volume work, Rudbeck traced Atlantean influences in Norse myths as well as his own country's megalithic ruins. He concluded that a few Atlantean survivors had come to Sweden, contributing to its cultural development and laying the foundations – particularly in ship construction – for what would much later become the Viking Age (9th to 12th centuries CE).

Interestingly, during the early 1960s Swedish archaeologists identified Scandinavia's earliest known Bronze Age site in digs at Uppsala, Sweden. Radiocarbon testing revealed a habitation date of around 2200 BCE. Rudbeck stated that the Atlanteans arrived at Uppsala around 2400 BCE. This may be significant because it is supposedly the time of the Second Atlantean Flood, brought about by the near miss of a debris-laden comet in 2193 BCE (see pages 18–19).

Atlantean Scholarship

The man most responsible for bringing Atlantis to the attention of the wider public was Ignatius Donnelly (1831–1901), a U.S. congressman and founder of Atlantology. Donnelly's 1882 book *Atlantis, the Antediluvian World* was a

U.S. congressman Ignatius Donnelly was adamant in his belief that Atlantis really existed.

was highly influential in the growing field of Atlantology. His 1904 work *Cosmic Memory: Prehistory of Earth and Man* maintained that the Atlanteans formed one of humankind's "root races," a people who did not require speech, but communicated telepathically in images. According to Steiner, the story of Atlantis can be found repeated in Germanic myth. Steiner wrote that the Atlanteans were the first people to develop the concept of good versus evil, and laid the groundwork for all ethical and legal systems.

runaway bestseller. Within a few years of its release, it had sold out 23 American editions, and an additional 26 overseas editions. The book is still published in more than a dozen languages and remains a core textbook of Atlantology.

Rudolf Steiner (1861–1925), founder of the Steiner educational movement,

The work of popularizing Atlantis was later taken up by the Austrian physicist Otto Heinrich Muck (1883–1965). In his book *The Secret of Atlantis* (1965) he attempted to offer a scientific evaluation of Plato's account of Atlantis. Charles Berlitz (1913–2003) also helped revive popular interest in the subject with his books *The Mystery of Atlantis* (1974) and *Atlantis, the Eighth Continent* (1984). A talented linguist, Berlitz concluded that many modern and ancient languages derive from a single prehistoric source, which he traced to Atlantis.

THE DESTRUCTION OF ATLANTIS

The French astronomer G.R. Corli (1744–1806) was the first person to suggest that Atlantis was destroyed by an extraterrestrial impact. In 1785 he put forward the idea that a fragment from a passing comet collided with the Earth, causing a cataclysm that wiped out the legendary island. Nearly 100 years later, Ignatius Donnelly, in his book, *Ragnarok: Age of Fire and Gravel* (1884), also proposed that the island civilization had been annihilated by a comet's collision with the Earth.

Atlantis – Comets and Asteroids

In the 1920s and 1930s, Donnelly's theory was revived and supported by the German physicist Hans Hoerbiger (1860–1931), who believed that the Atlantean catastrophe could have occurred as the result of the Earth's impact with a cometary fragment of frozen debris. Immanuel Velikovsky (1895–1979), in *Worlds in Collision* (1950), elaborated on the possibility of a celestial impact as responsible for the sudden extinction of a pre-flood civilization.

Intriguing as these theories were, they were largely unsupported by physical evidence. But many Atlantologists believed physical evidence was found in 1964 when a German researcher, Otto Muck, announced his discovery of twin deep-sea holes in the ocean floor. According to Muck, they were caused by a small asteroid that split in half and set off a chain reaction of geological violence along the length of the Mid-Atlantic Ridge, a line of subsurface volcanoes to which the island of Atlantis was supposedly connected.

In the late 1980s and early 1990s, astronomers Victor Clube and Bill Napier put forward their "fire from heaven" theory to explain the destruction of Atlantis. According to them, the destruction came about not through a single collision but a bombardment of dozens or hundreds of small meteorites as our planet passed through or near a large cloud of debris from the disintegration of a giant comet.

Today, most Atlantologists believe the final destruction of Atlantis was caused by an extraterrestrial impact or series of impacts. They seek to link this explanation to the numerous traditions of a Great Deluge caused

It would have taken a truly huge disaster to obliterate Atlantis so completely.

the Great Flood was caused when a "planet" collided with the Earth.

Modern Support for the Meteor Theory

Scientific evidence suggests that comets passed dangerously close to the Earth around the years 3100, 2200, 1682 and 1198 BCE, with the first and especially the last event causing the most serious damage. These cometary close calls may have caused barrages of meteors to rain on the Earth, leading to mass death and the fundamental disruption of civilization.

by some celestial event, recounted by peoples on both sides of the Atlantic Ocean.

Evidence from Literature and Folk Memory

In Plato's *Timaeus*, the fall of an extraterrestrial object foreshadows the island's destruction.

Inscriptions on the walls of Medinet Habu (see page 23) in the Upper Nile Valley – the victory temple of Pharaoh Ramses III – tell how the "Sea People" invaders of Egypt were destroyed: "The shooting star was terrible in pursuit of them," before their island went under the sea.

Ibrahim ben Ebn Wauff Shah, Abu Zeyd el Balkhy and other Arab historians use the story of Surid, the ruler of a pre-flood kingdom, to explain that

LEGENDARY TALES

THE PLEIADES

In North America, the Cherokee Indians remembered Unadatsug, a group of stars – the Pleiades – one of which "creating a fiery tail, fell to Earth. Where it landed a palm tree grew up, and the fallen star transformed into an old man, who warned of coming floods." Similar accounts may be found among the Quiche Maya of the Lowland Yucatán, the Muysica of Colombia, the Arawak Indians of Venezuela, the Aztecs at Cholula, the ancient Greeks and in Jewish scriptures. According to the Jewish Talmud: "When the Holy One, blessed be He, wished to bring the Deluge upon the world, He took two stars out of the Pleiades."

In their 2000 book *Uriel's Machine*, authors Christopher Knight and Robert Lomas theorize that the direction of Earth's magnetic field was abruptly changed around 3150 BCE, when a comet struck the Mediterranean Sea. There is evidence of massive quantities of ash in the atmosphere around that time, documented through tree rings in Ireland and England. At the same time, there is evidence of widespread burning throughout various northern European bogs, and the Dead Sea may have risen by around 300 ft (92 m).

Multiple Impacts

Atlantologists argue that multiple impacts in the late fourth millennium BCE may have devastated Atlantis. There is evidence of volcanic eruptions and earthquakes from Iceland to the Azores, perhaps sparked by meteorites colliding with the geologically unstable Mid-Atlantic Ridge. These, they suggest, may have shattered much of the Atlantean capital, while tsunamis could have smashed into the island's coastal regions.

Atlantologists speculate that most survivors of the catastrophe rebuilt Atlantis, but many decided to migrate to other parts of the world at this time. This, they allege, explains the founding of civilization in Egypt, the Indus Valley, China and Mesoamerica, as well as the building of Britain's megalithic sites at Stonehenge, the Stones of Stenness,

Maes Howe, the Ring of Brodgar and Skara Brae in the Orkney Islands.

Historic accounts suggest a second calamity less than a thousand years later. Plato wrote in the Laws that the deluge of Ogyges occurred less than 2,000 years before his time; that is, around 2300 BCE. The Roman scholar Varo stated that it took place in about 2136 BCE. William Whiston, the 18th-century theologian, historian and mathematician, suggested that the near miss of a large comet caused the global flood of Noah in 2349 BCE. W. Bruce Masse, a 20th-century environmental archaeologist, found that "the period 2350–2000 BCE witnessed at least four cosmic impacts (c. 2345, 2240, 2188 and 2000 BCE) and perhaps a fifth (c. 2297–2265 BCE)." One of them, a 359-megaton asteroid, apparently exploded over Argentina, creating a series of craters across the Rio Cuarto area.

Atlantologists contend that a cataclysm in about 2193 BCE prompted a second wave of Atlantean migration to the Americas, North Africa, Western Europe and the Middle East.

Fire from Heaven

The penultimate global catastrophe was apparently longer in coming. Pre-Columbian Mexicans remembered it as Quihuitl, meaning "the Fire from Heaven," and it is depicted in its own square on the Aztec Calendar Stone as a sheet of descending flame. To the south, in Peru, the flood hero Thonapa arrived with his people after the Unu-Pachacuti, "the World Overturned by Water."

The priest-historian Manetho recorded that a "blast of God" prostrated Egypt, destroying large metropolitan centers such as Ithtaw ("Residence City") and Hetepsenusret. Dendrochronologist Michael Baillie has suggested that the plagues of Egypt referred to in the biblical book of Exodus were brought about by a severe climate regression due to volcanic ash filling the atmosphere and the effects of a comet's pass near the Earth. He cites German, British, Irish and North American tree rings as evidence of prodigious ash fall.

Atlantologists date this disaster to around 1628 BCE. They claim Atlantis again suffered significant damage from earthquakes and tsunamis, although on a smaller scale than on the two previous occasions.

LOST WORLD FILES

THE AGE OF TAURUS

The 1628 BCE cataclysm drew a line in history, separating the Old from the Middle Bronze Age. It was during the period that followed, until the end of the Late Bronze Age in about 1200 BCE, that Plato set his account of Atlantis. According to astrologers, the late 17th century BCE also marks the end of the Age of Taurus. Atlantologists believe that these astrological ages were known to the Atlanteans, who celebrated the passing of this age with the ritual slaughter of bulls, pointing out Plato's reference to this practice in his account of Atlantis. In many other later cultures, such as the Minoans, Mycenaeans, Hittites, Trojans and Assyrians, bull sacrifice was regarded as a prelude to renewal in the rhythm of growth. The Atlanteans may also have intended it as an appeal to their god Poseidon against a recurrence of the catastrophe of 1628 BCE.

Could the Aztec Calendar Stone hold the key to understanding the fate of Atlantis?

The Final Impact

According to Atlantologists, reconstruction of Atlantis proceeded immediately after the 1628 BCE disaster, resulting in the capital's most opulent phase. But it was not to last. The cataclysm of 1198 BCE was, allegedly, the most devastating of all, destroying Atlantis and shutting down the entire Bronze Age. Swedish geologists Thomas B. Larsson and Lars Franzen write that "relatively large extraterrestrial bodies hit somewhere in the eastern North Atlantic, probably on the shelf of the Atlantic coast of North Africa or southern Europe, around 1000–950 BCE, mainly affecting the Mediterranean parts of Africa and Europe, but also globally."

Some Atlantologists believe that the island of Atlantis itself may have been struck by one of these "large extraterrestrial bodies." W. Bruce Masse cited a "locally catastrophic terrestrial impact around 1000 BCE" that occurred in the badlands of northern Montana. West of Broken Bow, Nebraska, lies a 1-mile (1.6-km) wide impact crater created approximately 3,000 years ago by a meteor that exploded with the equivalent force of a 120-megaton nuclear blast. Greenland's Camp Century ice-cores reveal that a global disaster threw several thousand cubic kilometers of ash into the atmosphere in about 1170 BCE.

The Harris Papyrus documented immense clouds of ash overwhelming the Nile Valley from the west at the time of Ramses III's coronation in 1198 BCE. Soon afterward, he defended Egypt from an invasion of the "Sea People," who told his scribes that a "shooting star" burned their homeland before it sank into the sea.

Atlantologists continue to debate the exact nature of the catastrophe that destroyed the legendary civilization.

Geologist Robert Hewitt described the end of the Bronze Age as one of the worst catastrophes in history. Larsson and Franzen felt compelled by the geological evidence to propose that "cosmic activity could offer an explanation for the observed changes. We even suggest that relatively large asteroids or comets – about 0.3 miles (0.5 km) in diameter – hit somewhere in the eastern Atlantic."

Volcanoes and Tsunamis

Vulcanism around the world peaked at the close of the 13th century BCE. Italy's Mount Vesuvius exploded on three separate occasions during the century after 1200 BCE. Large-scale eruptions occurred in Arabia, Russia, Japan, North America and Central America. In the Atlantic, volcanoes erupted in Iceland, Ascension Island, Candlemas, the Azores and the Canaries.

Development of Stonehenge terminated around this time and the site was abandoned, while Bavaria's Black Forest went up in flames. Across Scandinavia, most coastal regions were evacuated. Large areas of low-lying land, including the Hungarian Plain, were deluged. Coastal waters surged over the southeastern regions of North America. This catastrophic inundation seems to have been triggered by meteor and asteroid falls in the Atlantic Ocean, as indicated by a pattern of impact craters, or "bays," in

LOST WORLD FILES

GLOBAL FLOODING

Between 1200 and 1000 BCE, there was surge in lake levels around the world. New lakes formed in Germany near Memmingen, Munich, Ravensburg and Toelz. In the German Rhineland a vast majority of oak trunks show signs of flooding around 1000 BCE. Lakes, such as Loughbashade in Northern Ireland, overflowed. In North America, Utah's Great Salt Lake and Canada's Waldsea Basin reached abnormally high levels. So did South America's Lake Titicaca in the Bolivian Andes and Lago Cardiel in western Argentina. The world's largest soda lake, Turkey's Lake Van, rose 253 ft (77 m) in two years. Climatologists calculate that such an increase would have required approximately 150 in (381 cm) of rainfall.

South Carolina. Earthquakes and fires devastated Athens, Mycenae, Tiryns, Knossos, Troy, Urgarit and Cyprus. The imperial capital of the Hittite Empire, Hattusas, was consumed by fire.

Perhaps around this time, Mount Atlas also detonated in a series of ferocious eruptions, then collapsed into the sea. "In a single day and a night," according to Plato, Atlantis was obliterated. Atlantologists speculate that those who survived the final Atlantean destruction fled to various parts of the world, and these new arrivals have been remembered in the mythic traditions of their hosts.

THE LEGACY OF ATLANTIS

According to Atlantologists, the legacy of Atlantis can be found in the early civilizations of North Africa, Europe and the Americas. Atlantologists theorize that all of these civilizations owed their rise to the influence of Atlantean refugees, who came to these places when their homeland was destroyed.

Rise of Egyptian Civilization

The Nile Valley was originally inhabited by a low-density population of scattered hunter-gatherers and fishermen living in small, disconnected groups along the river banks, where they dwelt in tiny clusters of one-room, stick-built huts. Their primitive way of life continued unchanged for thousands of years.

Then, in 3100 BCE, Egypt began its swift rise to a sophisticated civilization that built temples, developed a written language and excelled in science, engineering and the arts. Atlantologists have argued that this relatively abrupt transformation can only have come about due to external influence. As evidence they point to discoveries made in the mid-20th century in the Sahara Desert.

Some authors have claimed that the pyramids had the original function of transforming seismic energy into electricity.

Saharan Culture

In 1955, geologists working in the Sahara retrieved core samples that proved the region had been fertile enough to support herds of cattle as recently as 3000 BCE. Only in the decades after that, they claimed, did North Africa begin to lose its battle with the advancing sands. At around the same time, archaeologists discovered the first evidence of a nomadic people who inhabited the Sahara. The Pastoralists, as archaeologists came to refer to this ancient people, appeared to share numerous features with Egyptian civilization.

Illustrations have been found at Jabbaren and Aouanrhet in the Sahara, painted with the same red ocher the Egyptians used in their temple wall murals. They show women wearing wreaths and headdresses identical to those in the Nile Valley. Paintings at Tassili-n-Ajjer, in the Oran Province of Libya, show girls with Egyptian facial features, wearing Egyptian-style robes and Wadjet tiaras – Wadjet was a cobra goddess, protector of the Lower Nile.

The figures appear with the palms of their hands raised in the Egyptian manner of worship before animal-headed gods. The gods portrayed most often are the lion, falcon and cow, the latter sporting a lunar disk between her horns. In Egyptian religion, these beasts were Sekhmet, the goddess of fiery destruction, Heru (or Horus), the god of kingship, and Mehurt, whose name means "the Great Flood." These three are perhaps the most ancient gods in the Egyptian pantheon. They existed before Egypt's dynastic period and were said to have arrived "from the West."

Atlantologists propose that these Pastoralists were the dynastic Egyptians' own immediate ancestors, migrating eastward into the Nile Valley following the devastation of their Atlantean homeland. No pyramids have yet been discovered in the Sahara. The Atlantologists explain this by the fact that the wandering refugees saw the approach of the desert and realized the Sahara was becoming increasingly unsuited to permanent habitation.

Seeker's Account

THE MOST ANCIENT OF MEN

According to the first-century-BCE Greek geographer Diodorus Siculus:
"The Egyptians themselves were strangers who in very remote times settled on the banks of the Nile, bringing with themselves the civilization of their mother country, the art of writing and a polished language. They had come from the direction of the setting sun, and were the most ancient of men."

LOST WORLD FILES

THE GREAT PYRAMID

The Atlantologists theorize that Egyptian civilization was the result of a blending of native Egyptian culture with that of the technologically advanced Atlanteans. One of the most outstanding features of Egyptian civilization is the Great Pyramid at Giza. Atlantologists believe that the pyramid was built as a co-operative effort between Egyptian residents, who formed the labor force, and Atlantean architects.

For evidence of this, Atlantologists point to Arab histories, which state that the Great Pyramid's grand architect was Thaut, the Egyptian god of literature and science, the divine patron of learning and keeper of the ancient wisdom. According to ancient myth, Thaut arrived at the Nile Delta before the beginning of Egyptian civilization, carrying with him a body of knowledge preserved on "emerald tablets" from a flood that overwhelmed his homeland in the primeval sea. Some ancient writers described Egypt as the "daughter of Poseidon," the alleged creator of Atlantis.

The Atlantologist Alexander Braghine stated: "In the solution of the problem of the origin of the pyramid builders is hidden also the solution of the origin of Egyptian culture and of the Egyptians themselves."

War Between Atlantis and Egypt

Plato's *Timaeus* and *Kritias* describe the war between Atlantis and Egypt. Atlantologists conjecture that this conflict may have taken place in 1190 BCE. In that year, Egypt under Ramses III, the 20th-Dynasty pharaoh, was invaded by the Meshwesh or "Sea People."

The story goes that the Sea People's navy brushed aside Egyptian defenses at the mouth of the Nile delta and its troops stormed ashore and captured several major cities. Ramses withdrew his forces and regrouped, observing how the invaders advanced with their ships, which they relied upon for support. At the southernmost end of the Nile Delta, Ramses threw virtually all of his surviving naval units against the Sea People. The invaders' vessels not only outclassed the much smaller Egyptian craft, but outnumbered them. On the verge of being overwhelmed, Ramses' warships suddenly turned and fled, with the whole invading fleet in hot pursuit.

Ramses' smaller vessels lured their enemies into narrower, shallower stretches of the river, familiar to the Egyptian captains but unknown to the Sea People. The invaders found themselves unable to maneuver and began grounding on undetected shoals. The Egyptians now attacked the Sea Peoples' warships with a barrage of fire-pots, just as thousands of archers suddenly appeared along the shore to launch unremitting flights of arrows at the outmaneuvered invaders. Cut off from their floating supplies, the Sea People troops were routed up the delta towards its Mediterranean shores, and forced to flee in their remaining ships.

This artist's impression shows Ramses III leading Egyptian archers in repelling an attack on the Nile Delta by "Sea People" from Atlantis.

Egypt's Victory

But the war was far from over. The invasion had consisted of a three-pronged attack from the north against the delta, westward across Libya and at the Egyptian colony of Syria in the east. Infantry held the Libyan assault at Fortress Usermare, near the Egyptian frontier, until Ramses was able to bring up his forces, enduring terrible losses before managing to drive back the invaders. Ramses met the invaders on the beaches at Amor, where they suffered their final defeat. The pharaoh personally participated in this last battle, drawing his great bow against the invaders.

Ramses celebrated Egypt's victory by raising a temple, Medinet Habu, in West Thebes. On its walls he documented the progress of the war in illustrations and hieroglyphics. Atlantologists point out that this war came eight years after Atlantis was allegedly obliterated by a natural catastrophe. The "Sea People" may have been Atlanteans looking for a new homeland in which to settle.

The wall texts at Medinet Habu explain that Sekhmet, the goddess of fiery destruction, "pursued (the Sea People) like a shooting-star" and incinerated their homeland, which immediately thereafter "vanished beneath the waves." The Sea People's capital city was referred to as Neteru, meaning a sacred place. Plato also characterized Atlantis as "sacred."

Jaén

Near the southern Spanish city of Jaén are the remains of an ancient city. On finding it, archaeologists were surprised by the size of the buried site, but also by its layout, which was unlike any they had seen before. The city had been laid out in concentric circles of alternating canals separating artificial land rings. At the center was a small central island big enough to accommodate a village, but more likely used as a sacred acropolis. The moats were of varying width and depth, larger as they moved out from the ceremonial center.

The archaeologist Georgeos Díaz-Montexano wrote: '... the whole city was built with this model or original design from the first moment, as if its architects were already familiar with this circular concentric arrangement – which is apparent from the relative speed with which the city was built.'

Díaz-Montexano has pointed out that the ruined bases of towers, which are spaced at regular intervals around the perimeter, have similar circular and semicircular designs to examples at

An artist's impression of Atlantis.

another Andalusian site, the Neolithic fortress of Los Millares. The Jaén towers must have been particularly tall, judging from their broad foundations and the abundance of rubble resulting from their collapse. Díaz-Montexano was particularly surprised to observe that the entire archaeological zone displayed advanced construction techniques with mortared stonework extensively combined with adobe brick.

The Spanish City of Rings

Atlantologists have noted the unmistakable resemblance of the site at Jaén to Plato's description of Atlantis. Furthermore, human remains found there have been dated to between 2470 BCE and 2030 BCE. This period coincides with a global cataclysm that is said to have befallen Atlantis in 2193 BCE. This would tie in with Plato, who said that an Atlantean ruler called Gadeiros established a kingdom in Spain following that catastrophe. Archaeologial evidence suggests that the Jaén location was badly damaged and abandoned with great suddenness some time before 1500 BCE, about the time when another natural catastrophe apparently swept the world. Rebuilding began after 1200 BCE when a new population took up residence – survivors, perhaps, from the final destruction of Atlantis in 1198 BCE.

Atlantologists point out that in its five artificial islands and six moats, the Jaén site incorporates what they believe were the sacred numerals of Atlantis – five and six. Florida-based Atlantologist Kenneth Caroli argues: "The plan (for the city) did not develop gradually, but instead was present from the beginning, as if working from a known model since lost."

The Romans called this strange place Auringis, from the Greek Ouringis, although neither Romans nor Greeks were its builders. Díaz-Montexano speculates that Auringis or Ouringis translates into "city of the rings," from an ancient Indo-European word meaning the "Ring."

LOST WORLD FILES

THE LADY OF ELCHE

Further evidence that Auringis may have been an Atlantean colony can be found 200 miles (318 km) away at Elche, near Valencia, where a life-size terracotta sculpture of a woman was excavated. The "Lady of Elche" was carved with a high degree of skill and dates to some pre-Roman epoch. The woman's facial characteristics and her clothing appear to belong to a sophisticated, affluent people previously unknown to archaeology. Atlantologists point out that the sculpture was discovered in an area of Spain mentioned by Plato as the Atlantean kingdom of Gadeiros, and the slight slant of the subject's eyes is supposedly an Atlantean racial characteristic.

Basques – Descendants of Atlantis?

The Basque people are the long-time inhabitants of the Pyrenees regions, where they were known to Roman historians as the Vascones. Basque folk tradition speaks of the Aintzine-Koak (literally, "Those Who Came Before"), their prehistoric forefathers, remembered as the inhabitants of "Atlaintika." They were supposed to have sailed from the sunken "Green Isle," a powerful maritime nation that sank into the Atlantic Ocean after a terrible cataclysm and from which a few survivors reached the Bay of Biscay, eventually bringing the holy relics of their mysterious religion to the Pyrenees.

"Basque" is actually the word used by the English and French to describe a people who refer to themselves as the Euskotarak. The Basque call their language Euskara. It is a unique tongue, unrelated to any Indo-European language. Interestingly, Euskara shares some affinity with Finno-Urgic Patumnili (spoken in ancient Troy), Etruscan (spoken by the pre-Roman inhabitants of western Italy), Guanche (spoken by the indigenous population of the Canary Islands) and Nahuatl (spoken by the Aztecs). These long-dead languages are themselves only very imperfectly understood today. But Atlantologists believe it is significant that Basque Euskara contains similarities to the languages of four other peoples they regard as descendants of the Atlanteans. Some Atlantologists even speculate that Euskara may be the same tongue as was spoken in that lost world more than 3,000 years ago.

The Sacred Mounds of Atalia

"Atalya" is the name of an ancient ceremonial mound in Biarritz, Basque country. It is also a sacred mountain in the valley of Mexico venerated by the Aztecs. "Atalaia" is a site in southern Portugal featuring Bronze Age tumuli, or domed tombs, dating to the 13th century BCE, toward the end of the period when Atlantis is said to have flourished. "Atalya" is also a place in Gran Canaria, where pyramids built by the Guanches can still be seen. They were constructed in black, white and red volcanic stone, the same materials used by the Atlanteans, according to Plato.

The name "Italy" derives from "Atalia," when – according to Etruscan tradition –

LOST WORLD FILES

DOG WORSHIPPERS

The Canaries got their name from the Romans because of their custom of dog worship (*canis* is Latin for "dog"). Atlantologists see a link between this and the ancient Egyptian cult of Anubis, the dog-headed god – both peoples, according to Atlantologists, were descended from the Atlanteans.

Atlas ruled there in prehistory. "Italy" means literally the "Domain of Atlas," whose daughter was Atlantis. Indeed, this seems to be the meaning of "Atalia" whenever and wherever it was used, even by such widely diverse and otherwise unrelated peoples as the Basque, Guanches, Aztecs and Etruscans. Atlantologists argue that this implies a common ancestry – that all of these cultures were influenced earlier in their history by people from Atlantis. "Atalia," Atlantologists say, carries the same meaning in Euskara, Nahuatl, Iberian and Guanche – it describes a sacred mound or mountain. Perhaps the word "Atalia" refers back to Atlantis itself, where the holy mountain of Atlas was at the center of the empire's mysterious religious cult.

Is it possible that the Egyptian god Anubis had a precursor in the form of an Atlantean canine deity?

The Guanches

The Guanches were native inhabitants of the Canary Islands. They were discovered by Portuguese explorers in the mid-15th century, but then virtually wiped out by the Spaniards through wars and disease. The Guanches' chief deity was similar to Atlas, and was known to them as Ater. They told the Portuguese that their islands were, in ancient times, part of a larger homeland engulfed by the sea, a cataclysm their forefathers survived by climbing to the top of Mount Teide, Tenerife's great volcano. In his book, *Tois Aethiopikes* (45 CE), Roman geographer Marcellus records: "the inhabitants of the Atlantic island of Poseidon preserve a tradition handed down to them by their ancestors of the existence of an Atlantic island of immense size of not less than a thousand stadia (about 116 miles (185 km)), which had really existed in those seas, and which, during a long period of time, governed all the islands of the Atlantic Ocean."

The Olmecs

Mesoamerican civilization developed swiftly, much as it did in the Nile Valley. For at least 20,000 years, Middle America was populated by tribes of hunter-gatherers, whose material level of culture did not extend beyond primitive weapons and a few crude tools. Then, in 1500 BCE, a sophisticated, powerful civilization arose on both the Atlantic and Pacific coasts, spreading rapidly through much of Mexico.

Archaeologists refer to this first American civilization as Olmec, although it is a name of scientific convenience only, as no one knows what these people called themselves. The Olmecs introduced literacy, sculpture, monumental architecture, textile production, astronomy, calendars, a complex religion, government, social stratification, commerce, systems of weights and measures and divisions of labor. Atlantologists have argued that the civilization appeared as if from nowhere, in its entirety, as though imported from somewhere outside Mexico.

Further evidence of the Olmecs' non-native origins, they say, can be seen in Olmec sculptural art. These, they point out, portray non-Amerindian faces, including bearded men with Middle Eastern features, Asians bearing strong resemblances to modern Cambodians, and West Africans depicted in colossal stone heads.

Around 1200 BCE the Olmecs experienced an abrupt surge in population and reached the height of their influence. Thereafter they entered into a slow decline, eventually merging into the next stage of Mesoamerican civilization.

The Maya

The Maya arose in the Lowland Yucatán in about 400 BCE, and although clearly influenced by the Olmecs before them, they developed their own distinctive culture of city-states. Long assumed to have been a people of peaceful astronomer-priests, recent translation

Seeker's Account

A PLACE CALLED PATULAN

The *Books of Chilam Balam,* an 18th-century collection of Mayan legends, tells of those who crossed the ocean from Patulan to Mexico:

"… the wise men, the Nahuales, the chiefs and leaders, called U Mamae (the Old Men), extending their sight over the four parts of the world and over all that is beneath the sky, and, finding no obstacle, came from the other part of the ocean, from where the sun rises, a place called Patulan. Together these tribes came from the other part of the sea, from the east, from Patulan."

Could the monumental sculpted heads of the Olmecs in Mexico have been influenced by Lemurian culture?

of Mayan glyphs paints a completely different portrait. The Mayan city-states were engaged in ceaseless warfare with each other for control of territory and trade. They also engaged in human mutilation and sacrifice, although not on the scale of the later Aztecs. Various reasons have been put forward for the collapse of the Maya and the mass abandonment of their cities in about 900 CE. These include political revolution, collapse of trade routes, ecological disaster, epidemic disease and drought.

Of the daughters of Atlas in classical mythology – the seven Pleiades – one name is particularly evocative: Maia.

Atlantologists believe there may be a link between the nymph of Greek myth and the ancient Maya of Yucatán. Intriguingly, Yucatán's first city, Mayapan – from which the people derived their name – was founded by Chumael-Ah-Canule, the "First after the Flood," according to *The History of Zodzil*, a 16th-century collection of Mayan oral history. He escaped the Hun Yecil – the "Drowning of the Trees" – that engulfed Patulan, his kingdom on a large island across the Atlantic Ocean.

Images of Patulan's Destruction

At the top of the so-called Acropolis at the Mayan ceremonial city of Tikal in Guatemala, there used to be a sculpted frieze. The frieze was a portrayal of significant events in the history of the Maya up to the end of the ninth century, when the site was abandoned. The frieze began with the image of a man rowing his boat away from an island hurling its city into the sea during a volcanic eruption, while a corpse floats on the waters in between him and the doomed island of Patulan. When Teobert Maler (1842–1917), the great Austrian archaeologist and explorer, found

LOST WORLD FILES

BACABS AT CHICHEN ITZA

The Bacabs were mythical white-skinned rulers of the Maya who (similar to the Atlantean kings described by Plato) held up the sky, like a race of Atlases. According to Mayan legend, a great flood drowned most of the Bacabs. At Chichen Itza, the Mayan ceremonial center in Yucatán, is the Pyramid of the Feathered Serpent. On the walls inside the shrine at the top are the likenesses of four bearded Bacabs, signifying the four cardinal directions, as they support the sky. They wear a large conch shell on their backs, perhaps to represent their maritime origins, and their appearance has been described as European.

the Tikal frieze, he exclaimed, "Until that moment, I dismissed Plato's Atlantis as nothing more than a Greek fantasy. But now I know he told the truth."

The Aztecs

The Aztecs dominated Mesoamerica from the 14th to the early 16th century. Archaeologists believe they entered the valley of Mexico as a small tribe from the north around 1320 CE, and built their city, Tenochtitlan. Within a few generations, it had grown to become the capital of a powerful empire. Atlantologists point out that Tenochtitlan, with its surrounding human-made lake, bisecting canals and Temple of Ehecatl at its center, bears similarity to Plato's description of Atlantis.

Just two centuries after establishing themselves, the Aztecs were annihilated by Spanish invaders. How just 200 conquistadors could overthrow an empire of millions cannot be explained merely by the superiority of European firearms. One possible reason was the superstition of the Aztec rulers and their suspicion that Hernán Cortés, leader of the conquistadors, was a god. Aztec legends told of a white-skinned, yellow-bearded visitor, Quetzalcoatl, who arrived over the sea from the east and, with his followers, founded Mesoamerican civilization. The Aztecs were never entirely sure if Cortés was Quetzalcoatl, or his direct descendant. Paralyzed by uncertainty, they were unable to resist the invaders effectively, despite their huge numerical advantage.

Quetzalcoatl

The Aztecs traced their origins to the Sunrise Sea, their name for the Atlantic Ocean. Their founding fathers were culture-bearers from far away Aztlan, portrayed in their birch-bark illustrations as a volcanic island to the east. The Aztec Calendar Stone shows a series of cataclysmic events in world history. One of these is a great flood, following which the yellow-bearded founding father, Quetzalcoatl, or the "Feathered Serpent," arrived to initiate civilization in Middle America. This appears on the Calendar Stone as a pyramid being engulfed by a deluge of water falling from an overturned bucket. It was from this last catastrophe that Quetzalcoatl arrived.

Ehecatl and Atlas

Tenochtitlan's Temple of Ehecatl was a pyramid of five steps, painted red, white and black and situated at the center of the city. Atlantologists point out the similarities with Atlantis, where five was allegedly a sacred number and the chief building materials were red, white and black stone. Inside the Aztec temple was a statue of the god Ehecatl, depicted as a man supporting the sky on his shoulders. Here, say Atlantologists, is a startling similarity to Atlas, and, so they say, the names of the two gods may ultimately even be derived from the same linguistic root. Indeed, Cieza de Leon, one of the conquistadors, even compared the Aztec capital to Atlantis.

Was the architecture of Tikal influenced by Atlantean ideas?

Giants in Horned Helmets

In southern Wisconsin there were two giant earthworks referred to by pioneers who travelled through the region during the 1830s as the "Man Mounds." They were depictions of water spirits that led the Wolf Clan, ancestors of the Winnebago or Ho Chunk Indians, to safety in North America after the Great Flood.

One of the geoglyphs still exists, although in mutilated form, on the slope of a hill in Greenfield Township, outside Baraboo. Road construction cut off his legs below the knees, but the figure is otherwise intact. The giant is 213 ft (65 m) long and 32 ft (10 m) across at his shoulders. He is oriented westward, as though striding from the east, where the Deluge was supposed to have occurred. His horned helmet identifies him as Wakt'cexi, the flood hero. The geoglyph is no primitive mound, but beautifully proportioned and formed. Increase Lapham, a surveyor who measured the earthwork in the mid-19th century, commented: "All the lines of this most singular effigy are curved gracefully, and much care has been bestowed upon its construction."

The other hill figure, also in Sauk County, about 31 miles (50 km) to the northwest, was drowned under several fathoms of river by a dam project in the early 20th century. Ironically, the water spirit that led the Ho Chunk Indians from a cataclysmic flood was itself the victim of another, modern deluge.

LOST WORLD FILES

DESCENDANTS OF LEMURIA?

The Chumash Indians, who lived in southern California's coastal areas and have their own Great Flood tradition, possess a strikingly Caucasian appearance and great seafaring skills, suggesting a different ancestry from most other North American native peoples. Interestingly, they incorporated the word "Mu" in their names for southern California's offshore islands, such as Santa Barbara, which the Chumash called "Limu." "Mu" was also used by them to describe things related to the sea, such as Pismu, today's Pismo Beach.

Wilmington Long Man and Cerro Unitas Giant

Atlantologists see similarities to the Wisconsin effigy in other overseas landforms. The 311-ft (95-m) Wilmington Long Man is another giant male figure, cut into the chalk face of a hill in southern England, about 6.2 miles (10 km) northwest of Eastbourne. It is dated to 2000–1200 BCE, which Atlantologists believe were the last centuries of Atlantis. The British hill figure was originally portrayed wearing a horned helmet, much like the Wisconsin giant, but this was obliterated in the early 19th century.

The Long Man of Wilmington is carved into the slopes of Windover Hill, northwest of Eastbourne, England.

Another geoglyph is located in the Atacama desert of Chile's coastal region. Known as the Cerro Unitas Giant, it is a staggering 394 ft (120 m) in length. It wears an elaborate rayed crown, which Atlantologists have likened to a horned helmet. Atlantologists believe that these three effigy mounds were probably created by a single people and depict a common theme – namely, the migration of survivors from the Atlantis catastrophe, led by men whose symbol of authority was a horned helmet. Atlantologists even point out a link with the Sea People who invaded Egypt during the early 12th century BCE (see pages 22–23), who were depicted in the wall art of Medinet Habu wearing horned helmets.

SPIRITS AT THE BOTTOM OF THE SEA

In southern New Mexico, the Navajo preserve a flood legend with – some say – a distinctly Lemurian flavor. In their legend, instead of a cataclysmic event, there is a gradual but inexorable encroachment of the waters upon the land of a former people whose spirits now reside in a great "lodge" at the bottom of the sea. Navajo sand-paintings contain descriptions of this event and the resulting migration. It might seem strange that a people living so far inland from the ocean would have such a legend, yet the Navajo are relative newcomers to the southwest. They arrived there some 300 years ago from their ancestral homeland along the British Columbian shores of the Pacific Northwest.

years old. They base this dating on the accumulation on the stone's surface of a light patina known locally as "desert varnish."

About 50 such maze stones have been identified throughout Orange, Riverside, Imperial and San Diego counties, and at least 14 examples of labyrinthine rock art have been found in the area of Palm Springs. All are within 150 miles (240 km) of each other and virtually every one is rectangular, although they vary in size, with the smallest about 4 in (10 cm) across. They are invariably located on boulder-strewn mountainsides and Atlantologists speculate that they may mark the remnants of a pilgrimage route to commemorate an important event in the distant past.

The maze itself is in the form of a swastika, a sacred symbol for numerous Native American tribes. Among the Hopi Indians, the hooked cross signifies the migration of their tribe from the east following a great flood that overwhelmed early humankind. However, it is not known if ancestors of the Hopi carved the Hemet Maze Stone. Atlantologists see a possible significance in the swastika's westward-oriented design.

Maze Stones and Swastikas

The Hemet Maze Stone is a gray boulder upon which has been carved a labyrinthine maze enclosed in a square 5 ft 6 in (1.7 m) to a side. The petroglyph is located on a mountainside just west of Hemet, California, some 90 miles (145 km) southeast of Los Angeles. Atlantologists claim the carving on the stone is between 3,000 and 4,000

Muyscas-Zuhe

The Chibchans were a people who lived in the high valleys surrounding Bogotá and Neiva in Colombia at

According to the Hopi Indians, Southern California's Hemet Maze Stone represents the migration of their ancestors into North America from the East.

the time of the Spanish Conquest. The Chibchans revered the memory of their founding father, Muyscas-Zuhe, and even referred to themselves as the Muysca in his honor. Atlantologists have remarked upon the similarity between the name Muyscas-Zuhe and Musaeus, the fifth monarch of Atlantis as listed by Plato. In the Chibchan language, Muysca means "Musical Ones," and in Greek, Musaeus means "Of the Muses," divine patrons of the arts, from which we get our word "music."

The Chibchans believed that Muyscas-Zuhe was born in the "Gilded One," a prosperous kingdom situated on an island far out into the Atlantic Ocean, where Bochica, a fair-skinned giant with a long beard, supported the sky on his shoulders. Growing tired of this burden, Bochica accidentally dropped it one day, causing the Earth to be consumed in flames, then deluged by a great flood.

According to Chibchan tradition, Muyscas-Zuhe escaped from his homeland before it was engulfed by the sea, eventually landing on the shores of Colombia. There he shared the wisdom of his lost birthplace with the Chibchans, who knew him as the "Civilizer," and the "White One." After teaching the Chibchans how to live in an organized society, Muyscas-Zuhe departed for the distant Andes Mountains to bring similar enlightenment to the Incas' ancestors. Before leaving, he appointed a quartet of select chiefs to govern through his authority and example. Chibchan legend records that after the global fire and flood, Bochica reassumed his burden of the heavens, which he continues to support, but still causes earthquakes whenever he shifts the weight on his shoulders.

Atlantologists point out that the Chibchan mythology is remarkably similar to Plato's account of Atlantis. Bochica is the Colombian version of the first king of Atlantis, Atlas, depicted in Greek myth as a bearded titan holding up the sky. The event Bochica unleashed by dropping the sky sounds very much like the disaster – perhaps the collision of a comet with Earth – that triggered the destruction of Atlantis.

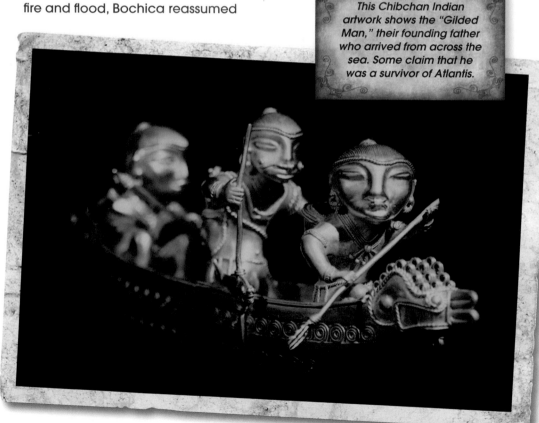

This Chibchan Indian artwork shows the "Gilded Man," their founding father who arrived from across the sea. Some claim that he was a survivor of Atlantis.

The "Gilded One"

This catastrophe was commemorated by the Chibchans in their most important ceremony, Calena-ma-noa. This translates as the "Water of Noa," giving it a striking resemblance to the Old Testament flood hero, Noah. During the ceremony, each newly installed Zipa (chief) demonstrated his lineage from Muyscas-Zuhe by coating his naked body in gold dust, applied with sticky resin, to represent the sunken homeland. He then jumped into the waters of Guatavita, a sacred lake outside Bogotá. The trail of gold dust that washed off his body during his dive signified the riches of the "Gilded One" lost at sea. The Zipa was then dressed in a blue robe, similar to azure raiment supposedly worn by the kings of Atlantis, as described by Plato.

Atlantologists add another layer of significance to all this. They point out that Lake Guatavita is, in fact, an astrobleme, a crater caused by a meteor fall that has since filled with water. Although the date of the crater's formation is uncertain, Atlantologists believe that the impact that created Guatavita may have occurred at a similar time to cometary events responsible for the destruction of Atlantis. In other words, the Chibchans may have recognized the crater-lake as being caused by the same celestial catastrophe memorialized in their "Water of Noa" ritual.

Other South American Flood Heroes

Venezuela's Orinoco Indians told 16th-century Spanish friars that Shikiemonu, the sky god, long ago caused the "Great Water," a worldwide flood, to drown the first humans, who had transgressed his sacred laws. Sharing pre-Columbian Venezuela with the Orinoco were the Carib Indians. They recalled the story of Amaicaca, their own deluge hero, who escaped the natural catastrophe in a "big canoe." It settled at the top of Mount Tamancu after the floodwaters receded.

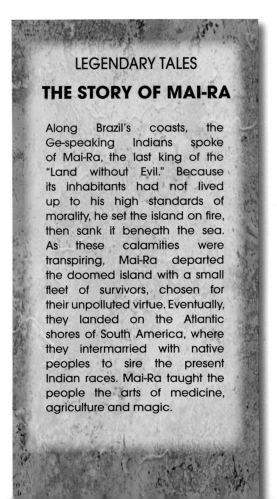

LEGENDARY TALES

THE STORY OF MAI-RA

Along Brazil's coasts, the Ge-speaking Indians spoke of Mai-Ra, the last king of the "Land without Evil." Because its inhabitants had not lived up to his high standards of morality, he set the island on fire, then sank it beneath the sea. As these calamities were transpiring, Mai-Ra departed the doomed island with a small fleet of survivors, chosen for their unpolluted virtue. Eventually, they landed on the Atlantic shores of South America, where they intermarried with native peoples to sire the present Indian races. Mai-Ra taught the people the arts of medicine, agriculture and magic.

Among the Maidu Indians of the eastern Sacramento Valley and foothills in northeastern California, and the Pomo Indians residing on the California coast north of the greater San Francisco Bay area, Kuksu was the creator of the world, who long ago set it on fire with celestial flames in response to the wickedness of mankind. Before the entire Earth was reduced to a burned-out cinder, he extinguished the conflagration with an awful deluge. The Paraguayan Indian's flood hero was known as Zume, a name resembling the Chibchans' Muyscas-Zuhe (see pages 34–36).

White Man of the Sea Foam

Like Mexico's Aztecs, the Incas were the last manifestation of a culture that preceded them by thousands of years.

Although the term is now generally applied to the whole people, "Inca" originally applied only to the royal family that ruled Peru in the 15th and 16th centuries CE.

The Inca rulers claimed direct descent from a foreigner, At-ach-u-chu, who arrived in Bolivia long ago. He was described as a tall, fair-skinned, red-haired, bearded traveller from the east who landed on the shores of Lake Titicaca after surviving a terrible deluge. His indigenous hosts called him the "Teacher of all Things" and, according to legend, he was the founder of Inca civilization, giving them agriculture, religion, astronomy, weights and measures, social organization and government.

At-ach-u-chu was the oldest of five brothers, the Viracochas, or "white men," and was himself more often referred to by his title, "White Man of the Sea

The Mataco flood legend describes a "rain of fire" causing terrible devastation.

LEGENDARY TALES

RAIN OF FIRE

The Mataco were Argentine Indians of the Gran Chaco. Their flood myth described "a black cloud at the time of the flood that covered the whole sky. Lightning struck and thunder was heard. Yet the drops that fell were not like rain. They fell as fire."

Foam," Con-tiki-Viracocha. "Sea foam" could perhaps have been a poetic description of the wave at the bow of his ship that brought him over the sea following a disastrous flood that drowned his homeland.

Holes Filled with Sacred Water

Atlantologists point out the similarity between At-ach-u-chu and Atcha, a term for the "Field of Reeds," remembered by the ancient Egyptians as a far-off, splendid but vanished city (possibly Atlantis). Atlantologists speculate that At-ach-u-chu might therefore mean the "Man from Atcha (Atlantis)." Indeed, At-ach-u-chu's myth places his birth in Yamquisapa, a rich and powerful island kingdom in the Atlantic Ocean that sunk to the bottom of the sea after having been set on fire

with a "celestial flame" for the idolatry of its sinful inhabitants.

This event was remembered as the Unu-Pachacuti, or "World Over-Turned by Water," a catastrophe of global proportions. It was commemorated at the Ushnu, a deep hole once located in Plaza de Armas, which is now the main plaza in Cuzco, Peru. It was into the Ushnu that the waters of the Unu-Pachacuti supposedly drained after the arrival of At-ach-u-chu. The hole was also regarded as an entrance to the sacred underworld. Inca worshippers would pour offerings of water, milk, fermented cactus juice, beer and other precious liquids down the Ushnu.

Interestingly, the ancient Etruscans of western Italy attached a similar significance to holes sited at the midpoints of their cities, such as Tarquinia and Populonia. Each hole was called a *mundus*, where holy water commemorating the Deluge was ritually deposited. The same kind of subterranean offerings were made at the ancient Greek festival of Hydrophoria and by the Phoenicians at Hierapolis in Syria. Among the Anasazi, Hopi and other native peoples of the North American southwest, ritual players in an ancestral ceremony were doused with water as they tried to climb out of an underground chamber known as a *kiva*. They symbolized the "emergence" of survivors from the Great Flood.

TECHNOLOGY OF ATLANTIS AND LEMURIA

Modern writers and filmmakers have made extraordinary claims for technological sophistication in Atlantis and Lemuria. In H.G. Wells' *Men Like Gods* (1923) and Walt Disney's *Atlantis, The Lost Empire* (2001), Atlantean science embraced everything from genetic modification and electric elevators to aircraft and submarines.

Lost Science

Atlantologists believe they have uncovered tantalizing clues of a kind of "superscience" existing in deep antiquity. However most scientists and historians reject the idea of a technologically advanced,

Is it possible that peoples of the distant past could have had access to advanced technology?

prehistoric race, mainly because there is no archaeological evidence for this.

Atlantologists dispute the idea that a graph of human technological progress over time would show a constantly ascending line. They argue that there are many examples of ancient civilizations creating technologies that were then forgotten when their societies collapsed, only to be rediscovered hundreds of years later. However much of the ancient "technology" that they cite as evidence of this theory, many scientists argue, is also legendary. For example, Atlantologists purport that Mayan understanding of celestial mechanics was not matched until the late 20th century. They also argue that ancient Inca agricultural techniques yielded three times as much produce as farming methods employed in today's Peru.

When the story of Atlantis was being written by Plato in the fourth century BCE, some of his fellow Greeks were sailing in the *Alexandris*, a colossal ship supposedly more than 400 ft (120 m) in length, the dimensions of which would not be seen again for another 2,000 years. Another favorite example of Atlantologists is a pregnancy test allegedly performed by 18th-Dynasty Egyptians, which was not rediscovered until the 1920s. However, regardless of the dubious veracity of some of these claims, it is nonetheless true that many other skills and technologies have been lost with the fall of past civilizations, only to be rediscovered many centuries later.

LOST WORLD FILES

THE BAGHDAD BATTERY

In 1938, German archaeologist Dr. Wilhelm Koenig was making an inventory of artifacts at the Iraq State Museum in Baghdad when he became intrigued by a collection of 2,000-year-old clay jars. Each of the jars contained a copper cylinder capped at the bottom by a copper disk and sealed with asphalt. Koenig was struck by their resemblance to a series of modern, dry-cell storage batteries. After the Second World War, Willard Gray, a technician at the General Electric High Voltage Laboratory in Pittsfield, Massachusetts, built an exact reproduction of the Baghdad jars. He found that, when filled with citric acid, an iron rod inserted into the copper tube generated 1.5 to 2.75 volts of electricity. It was not much, but sufficient to, for example, electroplate an object with gold. His experiment demonstrated that practical electricity might possibly have been applied to metalworking by ancient craftsmen.

Atlantologists speculate that the "Baghdad Battery" was probably not the first of its kind, but offered a glimpse of a hitherto unsuspected ancient technology – a technology that may have included far more impressive feats of electrical engineering long since lost.

Ancient Aviators

The first documented aerial voyages took place even before Plato was born, when a fifth-century BCE scientist, Archytas of Tarentum, invented a leather kite large enough to carry a young boy. In the earliest known example of aerial reconnaissance, the high-flying young man actually served as an observer for Greek armies on campaign.

Atlantologists conjecture that the technology of flight may have been mastered even further back in history. In 1898 a model was found in an Egyptian tomb near Sakkara in the Upper Nile Valley. It was labelled "bird" and catalogued Object 6347 at the Egyptian Museum in Cairo. Dr.

Khalil Massiha, examining the artifact in 1969, was startled to see that the "bird" not only had straight wings but also an upright tailfin. To Dr. Massiha, the object appeared to be that of a model airplane. It is made of wood, weighs 1.38 oz (39.12 g) and remains in good condition. The "aircraft's" length and wingspan are both 7 in (18 cm) and its nose is 1.25 in (3.2 cm) long. The extremities of the object and the wingtips are aerodynamically shaped. Apart from a symbolic eye and two short lines under the wings, it has no decorations, nor has it any landing legs.

In all, 14 similar flying models have been recovered from ancient digs in Egypt, dating from the Roman era back to the start of the Old Kingdom in the early third millennium BCE. The Sakkara specimen, for example, was retrieved from an archaeological zone identified with the earliest dynastic periods, at the very beginning of Egyptian civilization. This suggests that the model was not a later development, but belonged to the first years of civilization in the Nile Valley. Could these artifacts have been models of real flying machines, operated by the Egyptians' Atlantean forefathers? Many Atlantologists believe so.

LEGENDARY TALES

FLYING TEMPLE

In South America, the Andean flood hero Con-tiki-Viracocha (see page 39) – after accomplishing his civilizing mission among the Incas' ancestors – allegedly rose high into the air aboard a "temple" known as an Orichana, then vanished toward the setting sun. Interestingly, in Quechua, the Inca language, the word "Orichana" refers to something metallic and polished to a high sheen, so as to appear fiery. Orichana echoes Plato's orichalcum, the Atlanteans' high-grade copper that they used to adorn the walls of their capital city.

Vimana and Pauwvotas

There are references in the scriptures of ancient India to so-called Vimana aircraft, supposedly flown in ancient times. These appear in the epics

Ramayana, Mahabharata and Drona Parva. Other classic sources, namely the Vimaanika Shastra, Manusa and Samarangana Sutradhara, describe "aerial cars," which, they allege, were operating in prehistoric times.

Similarly, Hopi Indians of the North American southwest told of *pauwvotas* – airborne vehicles flown over immense distances by an ancestral people, before their beautiful island perished during a Great Deluge.

However, these alleged machines would have had little in common with modern aviation – there's no hint of how they were powered, since there are no references in the stories to anything resembling propellers, jet engines or other essential elements of aeronautics.

Atlantologists theorize that these folk memories of Vimanas, *pauwvotas* and the Orichana are all that remain of a lost Atlantean supertechnology that once, millennia before the Wright brothers, created some kind of aircraft.

Could the flying temples of the Hindu scriptures have been inspired by real Atlantean technology?

Building

Atlantologists believe that the Atlanteans excelled in the area of building, and that they may have spread those skills around the world. Could the ancient Egyptians have learned their building skills from Atlanteans? The Egyptians record that Thaut, survivor of the flood that brought his fellow "Followers of Horus" to the Nile Delta at the dawn of Egyptian civilization, was the Great Pyramid's chief architect.

Mining

The Menemonie Indians of North America's Upper Great Lakes region tell of the "Marine Men" – white-skinned people from across the Atlantic Ocean, who blasphemed against Mother Earth by "digging out her shiny bones." Atlantologists believe that this is a reference to copper miners who excavated more than 551,155,655 tons (half a billion tonnes) of the raw metal between 3100 and 1200 BCE. The miners were apparently able to determine the precise location of subterranean veins by dropping "magical stones" – known to the Menomonie as *yuwipi* – which made the copper-bearing rock "ring, as brass does." Could the pale-faced foreigners have been Atlanteans using their mining skills in North America?

This account from the Menemonie recalls a prospecting technique practiced by ancient European miners more than 3,000 years ago. Bronze with a high tin content – from one part in four to one in six or seven – emits a full, resonant sound when struck with a stone. Such bronze is today known as "bell metal" for the ringing tone it produces.

Seeker's Account

PLATO DESCRIBES THE WALLS OF ATLANTIS

"The entire circuit of the wall which went around the outermost one they covered with a coating of brass, and the circuit of the next wall they coated with tin, and the third, which encompassed the citadel, flashed with the red light of orichalcum (high-grade copper)."

Lemuria's "Wonder of the World"

According to the occultists who believe in the existence of Lemuria, that lost world had a more spiritual character than the materialistic Atlantis, and was less inclined toward technological innovation. Nevertheless, the occultists claim that Lemuria was responsible for the largest food factory ever constructed and one of humankind's greatest feats of engineering.

Today it is described as the "Eighth Wonder of the World" and it still exists

The extraordinary Banaue rice terraces have been described as the "Eighth Wonder of the World."

at Luzon in the Philippines, 156 miles (250 km) north of Manila. A tremendous stairway rises to 3,000 ft (915 m) above the valley floor, forming an ascending series of artificial plateaus for the growing of rice. From bottom to top, the stairway exceeds the height of the world's tallest skyscraper. The Banaue rice terraces, as they are known, cover more than 4,000 sq miles (10,360 sq km) of the Cordillera mountain range. If laid end to end, their paddies would form a line stretching halfway around the Earth. Even so, occultists believe

that less than 50 percent of the original agricultural network survives. They say that when they were functioning at their maximum capacity more than 2,000 years ago, the Banaue rice terraces yielded prodigious quantities of crops. This was not only due to their vast scale, but because of their highly efficient irrigation system fed by water from the rainforests above the terraces.

The occultists suggest that the Banaue rice terraces could have yielded enough food to feed several million people, and they imply the existence of a highly organized Pacific society during prehistory, currently unknown to archaeology.

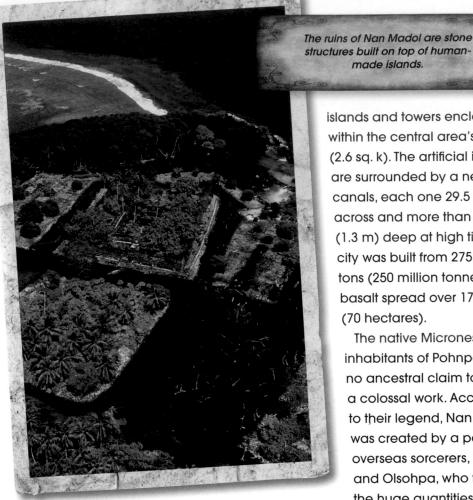

The ruins of Nan Madol are stone structures built on top of human-made islands.

islands and towers enclosed within the central area's 1 sq. m (2.6 sq. k). The artificial islands are surrounded by a network of canals, each one 29.5 ft (9 m) across and more than 4.25 ft (1.3 m) deep at high tide. The city was built from 275,577,828 tons (250 million tonnes) of basalt spread over 173 acres (70 hectares).

The native Micronesian inhabitants of Pohnpei make no ancestral claim to such a colossal work. According to their legend, Nan Madol was created by a pair of overseas sorcerers, Olsihpa and Olsohpa, who floated the huge quantities of stone

Nan Madol

Some 1,762 miles (2,820 km) east of the Banaue rice terraces lies the small island of Pohnpei. Off its northern shore stands an ancient ruined city that has been compared in scale to the Great Wall of China and the Great Pyramid of Egypt.

Built on a coral reef only 5.25 ft (1.6 m) above sea level, Nan Madol is a series of 92 rectangular human-made

through the air, a skill they learned in their homeland, Kanamwayso, before it was overwhelmed by a terrible catastrophe.

The city's sea walls are made up of basalt columns stacked like logs. The whole complex was originally surrounded by a wall 16 ft (5 m) high and 2,812 ft (857 m) long. Some existing ramparts are more than 13 ft (4 m) thick. The city's largest block, a single cornerstone of a tower, weighs 66 tons (60 tonnes). Despite the stone's impressive weight, it must have been raised, then set on a buried stone platform by the ancient builders.

Levitating Blocks

It has been estimated that 20,000 to 50,000 construction workers were needed to build Nan Madol. Its 5.5–28 ton (5–25-tonne) pillars of magnetized basalt were lifted to heights beyond 43 ft (13 m). The Micronesian legend that these blocks were levitated into position by ancient sorcerers recalls similar legends in other parts of the world.

According to Celtic traditions, the blocks of Stonehenge were raised by a similar kind of power. Greek myth records that in building the city of Thebes, Amphion lifted colossal blocks and fitted them into place through the music of his lyre. Likewise, North America's Ho Chunk Indians recount that the pyramidal mounds at the bottom of Wisconsin's Rock Lake were constructed through the power of communal song.

Occultists speculate that the spiritually powerful leaders of Lemuria were able to call upon such mysterious powers in the building of Nan Madol, as well as other structures, such as Easter Island's 110-ton (100-tonne) *moai* statues, Tonga's 116-ton (105-tonne) coral gate and Waimea Canyon's 23-ft (7-m) high Menehune Ditch on the Hawaiian island of Kauai.

LOST WORLD FILES

WHAT DO CONVENTIONAL SCHOLARS SAY ABOUT NAN MADOL?

According to conventional historians and archaeologists, the city was the capital of the Saudeleur Dynasty between about 500 and 1500 CE, which united Pohnpei's estimated 25,000 people. Excavations show that the area was occupied as early as 200 BCE. By the 8th or 9th century CE, islet construction had started, but the distinctive architecture using large blocks of stone was probably not begun until perhaps the 12th or early 13th century CE.

No one knows who built it. As well as the Pohnpeian myth about the sorcerers (see page 46), there is another local tradition that the builders of the Lelu complex on Kosrae (also composed of huge stone buildings) migrated to Pohnpei, where they built the even more impressive Nan Madol. However, radiocarbon dating indicates that Nan Madol predates Lelu.

Some possible quarry sites around the island have been identified, but how the stones were transported from the quarries to their current location is unknown. It has been suggested that they might have been floated via raft from the quarries. Certainly, the sea bed between the quarries and the island contains a trail of dropped stones. However, no one has successfully demonstrated or explained the process.

THE SEARCH FOR ATLANTIS

In March 2003, American psychologist Dr. Gregory Little and his wife, Lora, were trying to verify a strange sighting made eleven years earlier. They had been told of a wall-like structure lurking below 3.3 ft (1 m) of water in the Atlantic Ocean. The sunken enigma was said to lie near Andros Island, 150 miles (240 km) southeast of Miami, Florida. Andros is the largest island of the Bahamas, and also the greatest tract of unexplored land in the Western Hemisphere, thanks to its profuse, often impenetrable mangrove swamps.

The Littles were following up on the claims of a local dive operator, Dino Keller. In 1992 he claimed to have navigated his tour boat over a shallow coral reef, where he observed the underwater "wall" while cruising Nicolls Town Bay off the extreme northeast

What long-forgotten secrets could be hidden beneath the waters of the Atlantic Ocean?

end of the island. His description of the object as a "wall" was puzzling because archaeologists believe that Andros remained uninhabited until the 17th century, when former slaves from West Africa were stranded on the island. Today's 10,000 inhabitants, residing mostly in small towns along its eastern coast, are the descendants of these castaways.

Andros Platform

Following Keller's directions, the Littles snorkelled about 1,968 ft (600 m) from shore to find a 1,503-ft (458-m) long, 164-ft (50-m) wide arrangement of massive blocks in three, well-ordered sloping tiers, interspersed by two bands of smaller stones. Although standing 10 ft (3 m) beneath the surface, its top section was more than 3.3 ft (1 m) deep, just as described by Keller. Large stones comprising the tiers averaged 16 by 29 ft (5 by 6 m), and 3.3 ft (1 m) thick. Each of the three tiers was 56 ft (17 m) wide. The Littles also found a ramp leading from the floor of the harbor lagoon to the top of the platform.

The feature's regular appearance and almost uniformly square-cut blocks suggested to the Littles that it was made by humans. Given its location at a natural harbor in the North Atlantic Current, they thought it may have been a quay, breakwater or port facility of some kind.

LOST WORLD FILES

JOULTER CAYS DISCOVERY

Following the Littles' discovery of the Andros Platform, they and other investigators expanded their exploration of the waters around Andros. According to local traditions there existed another large underwater formation about 6 miles (10 km) north of the island in an uninhabited chain of islands known as the Joulter Cays. Here, Dr. Little and company found a stone wall at least 1,312 ft (400 m) long.

Although its uppermost tier rose to within just 7 ft (2 m) of the water surface, "the lowest tier of stones revealed more limestone blocks under the visible portion," Dr. Little stated. "How far down it extends (into the sea bed) is unknown." The blocks themselves appeared to have been cut into rectangles and squares, 3.3 to 6.6 ft (1 to 2 m) wide and about 3.3 ft (1 m) thick, though a few, less typical specimens were larger.

Only sections of the wall stood intact, but its human-made nature appeared evident to the explorers due to the regularity of the stonework and what they described as the unnatural placement of one block upon another. They concluded the site was a large public-works project built many thousands of years ago by an unknown civilization.

The structure contained a number of rectangular holes 5 in (13 cm) wide and deep, resembling post holes cut into some of the cyclopean stones just below the uppermost tier. The Littles speculated that these may have held mooring pylons used to tie up docked ships. Some investigators who have since studied the blocks have suggested they may have been quarried from local beach rock and deliberately set in place, a marine construction practice that was common throughout the ancient world.

But who could have built such a massive project at a time when territory now covered by the ocean was dry land? And were the Andros Platform and Joulter Cays wall the only structures of their kind in the vicinity or merely part of a much larger complex yet to be found?

Precise dating of the sunken structures is problematical, but Dr. Little believes the two structures are stylistically related and he estimates that the Andros Platform dates prior to 10,000 BCE. Sea levels were low enough then for its creation on dry land. Atlantologists point out that the Andros Platform has six alternating bands of stone. Six was the sacred numeral of Atlantis, whose city planners, according to Plato, incorporated the holy number in the capital's alternating stone walls.

The Bimini Road

Some 99 miles (160 km) northwest of Andros lies the small island of Bimini, also part of the Bahamas. The feature for which the island is best known today is the so-called "Bimini Road." This structure – only 20 ft (6 m) beneath the ocean surface – suggested a paved highway to early investigators, who observed its huge, square-cut blocks running in two straight lines, diverging across the sea bottom for about 2,083 ft (635 m).

Core samples drilled out of the Bimini Road revealed fragments of micrite,

LOST WORLD FILES

IS THE BIMINI ROAD NATURAL OR HUMAN-MADE?

Most conventional geologists believe the Bimini Road is a natural feature composed of beach rock that has broken up into a variety of shaped blocks. They say it is a peculiar result of sedimentation and wave erosion that can also be found in other parts of the world, including the Tessellated Pavement at Eaglehawk Neck, Tasmania. Atlantologists dispute this. They say that at the time of its formation (around 17,000 years ago, according to geologists), it stood well above sea level, so no wave erosion was possible. They also point to samples revealing fragments of micrite, which does not appear in beach rock, and granite, which is not native to the Bahamas. The arguments continue.

A deep-sea submarine equipped with state-of-the-art equipment dives into the seas around Bimini in search of evidence of Atlantis.

which does not occur in beach rock, and in 1995, divers at the Bimini Road found granite, which is not native to the Bahamas. The state of Georgia in the United States, hundreds of miles (km) away, is the closest source of granite. Moreover, adjacent stones in the road sometimes contain different geological components, such as aragonite and calcite. This, according to Atlantologists, is unlike the chemical uniformity of naturally occurring beach rock.

Atlantologists point to other pieces of evidence to bolster their argument for the artificiality of the Bimini Road. They say the stones that make up the "road" are not the same as the beach rock in shallow waters off the island's western shore. They describe the stones in the road as massive square-cut, pillow-like blocks fitted together, sometimes placed one atop another, that terminate in an unnatural-seeming J-shape. The natural beach rock, by contrast, is formed into roughly squarish flakes that are not neatly fitted together nor stacked on top of each other, but often overlap at their edges like – in the words of Atlantologist Frank Joseph – "a set of bad teeth."

Beach Rock or Paving Stones?

The natural beach rock of Bimini curves parallel to the shore. The Bimini Road, however, runs diagonal to Bimini's former ancient shoreline. Atlantologists believe it would be impossible for such an orientation to have formed under natural conditions.

Atlantologists have made detailed comparisons between natural beach rock and what they regard as the "paving stones" found in the Bimini Road. They have observed that beach rock comprises a single layer, compared to the three and four layers found in the paving stones. The former is only a little more than an inch (3 cm) thick, while the road's blocks are almost 3.3 ft (1 m) thick.

The road also contains what they describe as "several angular keystones" with "notches to fit into tenons." For Atlantologists, this recalls a prehistoric building style encountered in the Andean walls of Cuzco, Sacsahuaman and Machu Picchu. They also compare the Bimini Road to the ancient wall of Lixus on the Atlantic coast of Morocco,

Seeker's Account

WILLIAM DONATO

The Atlantologists base many of their assertions about the Bimini Road on research undertaken by a Californian archaeologist named William Donato. After more than 20 years of subsurface investigations, including scuba dives, sonar, underwater cameras and submarines, he is certain that the lost civilization has been found. "I not only believe that Bimini was Atlantis," Donato says, "I bet my life it was Atlantis."

During a November 2006 dive off the north shore of the island, Donato found what he believed to be an artificial construction 98 ft (30 m) beneath the surface of the sea. Dr. Greg Little, his colleague and the discoverer of the Andros Platform, reported that "the rectangular forms consist of elevated stone on the bottom that has been covered by thick layers of coral. Several

of the photos clearly show what seem to be building blocks, some of which are embedded vertically into the bottom. In short, these forms appear, at face value, to be building foundations of some kind. These rectangular forms lie uniformly on a ridge running for at least a mile (1.6 km), and a 10-foot (3-m) drop-off is adjacent to them. This drop-off leads to a narrow, flat area that then descends quickly."

Dr. Little adds that Donato's find occurred "about 10 feet (3 m) above the 10,000 BCE shoreline," which would place the structure near the close of the fourth millennium BCE. This rough dating persuades some Atlantologists that the underwater formations uncovered by Donato were human-made ruins from the early Bronze Age, an era of extensive seafaring, when Atlantis approached the zenith of its power and influence.

which is made of colossal blocks of square, unmortared stone perfectly fitted together. Atlantologists conjecture that the two structures were made by the same Atlantean civilization.

An Atlantean Outpost?

Despite the dramatic discoveries off Andros and Bimini, Atlantologists believe that the western Atlantic is an unlikely location for the capital of the lost civilization. Plato described the island of Atlas as mountainous, fertile, seismically unstable, populated by elephants and geographically situated to invade the Mediterranean World. None of these characteristics apply to the Bahamas. These formations are, in the opinion of most Atlantologists, more likely to be the remains of a western outpost of the Atlantean empire.

Atlantis researcher Vonda Osman is seen here with a block of stone removed from the Bimini Wall.

Nevertheless, Atlantologists are extremely excited by the discoveries. If Bimini is not exactly Atlantis, they say, it may nonetheless be the first example of Atlantean civilization found and recognized as such since its disappearance. For Atlantis itself, say Atlantologists, researchers would be better off looking elsewhere, beneath the waves of the northeast Atlantic.

The Horseshoe Seamounts

In 1949, a geologist named Dr. Maurice Ewing, aboard the research vessel *Glomar Challenger*, found an ocean-floor formation in the northeast Atlantic later dubbed the Horseshoe Seamounts. It comprised a large island ringed by a range of high mountains. Ewing determined that its highest peak, dubbed Mount Ampere, was a volcano that had collapsed beneath the sea within the past 12,000 years.

Atlantologists claim that the Horseshoe Seamounts fit the basic description of Atlantis set out in Plato's two dialogues: they comprise a ring of high mountains lying outside the Straits of Gibraltar; their foremost peak, Mount Ampere, stands to the south – the same position assumed by Mount Atlas. It is thought that Mount Ampere stood above sea level as an island until it collapsed beneath the surface within the past 10,000 years; the final

destruction of Atlantis is said to have taken place 3,200 years ago.

Core samples taken from the ocean floor more than 1.9 miles (3 km) deep came up with prodigious amounts of beach sand – physical evidence for a former shoreline that had been subject to untold centuries of wave action at sea level. This was evidence that the deep-ocean landmass had at one time, and for a very long period, been dry territory above sea level.

Atlantologists also point out that the estimated dimensions of the Horseshoe Seamounts – 322 miles

LOST WORLD FILES

ELEPHANT BONES

Plato's *Kritias* mentions that elephants once abounded on the island of Atlas. Critics have long scoffed at Plato for including this fantastically out-of-place animal in the middle of the ocean, far from its African and Asian homelands. But in 1960, oceanographers dredging the sea bottom of the Atlantic some 201 miles (322 km) off the Portuguese coast unexpectedly hauled up hundreds of elephant bones from more than forty different locations.

Scientists concluded that the elephants may, in ancient times, have wandered across a now submerged land bridge, extending from the Atlantic shores of Morocco into formerly dry land long since sunk beneath the sea. Atlantologists viewed this discovery as further evidence that Plato's Atlantis was indeed sited in the Atlantic Ocean.

(515 km) from west to east by 194 miles (310 km) from north to south – are in rough agreement with the dimensions Plato gives in the *Kritias* for the island of Atlas: 367 miles (588 km) from west to east by 228 miles (365 km) from north to south.

Diatoms

Less than ten years after Dr. Ewing's first discovery of the Horseshoe Seamounts and Mount Ampere, Stockholm's Riksmuseum launched a Swedish deep-sea expedition under the command of Dr. René Malaise, aboard the research vessel *Albatross*. From the ocean floor some 1.25 miles (2 km) beneath the surface of the Atlantic, the scientists brought aboard fossilized remains of several thousand diatoms – small algae that flourished over the past 12,000 years.

Dr. Malaise's palaeobiologist colleague R.W. Kolbe went on to catalogue more than 60 freshwater diatom species at depths of 0.6 mile (1 km) and deeper across the mid-Atlantic. These retrieved algae fossils would have once grown in freshwater lakes, suggesting that a large stretch of dry land was once located in today's open ocean.

According to Plato's writings, "There was (on the island of Atlantis) every kind of animal, domesticated and wild, among them numerous elephants."

LOST WORLD FILES

ROBOTS RETRIEVE ROCKS

Additional evidence that the Horseshoe Seamounts could once have been an island was uncovered in 1963 by Dr. Maria Klinova, an oceanographer for the Soviet Academy of Sciences. While investigating an area of the Horseshoe Seamounts on the *Mikhail Lomonsov*, Klinova's robotic devices scooped up several unusual rocks from the sea floor. Laboratory testing showed that the specimens had not been formed at the 1-mile (1.6-km) depths where they were found, but on dry land about 10,000 years ago.

These revelations have convinced Atlantologists that a large mountainous landmass somewhat smaller in area than Portugal – about 34,750 sq miles (90,000 sq km) – did in fact occupy the mid-Atlantic Ocean within the past 10,000 years. Most scientists, however, are unpersuaded that this island was the fabled lost kingdom of Atlantis. And they are likely to remain so until evidence of human-made structures are discovered on the ocean floor.

Ruins on Mount Ampere?

In March 1974, geologists and biologists aboard a Soviet research vessel, the *Academician Petrovsky*, probed the shallow waters off Morocco's northern coasts in order to study the topographical features of submerged mountain peaks, hoping to discover some unknown species of marine life. Their investigations were mostly conducted using sonar sweeps and subsurface photography. As the *Academician Petrovsky* cruised farther west over the Horseshoe Seamounts, deep-sea cameras inadvertently captured a series of images that appeared to resemble the partial remains of a ruined city. Ivanovich Marakuev, an underwater-photography specialist on board the ship, confirmed that they resulted from neither film nor instrument anomalies or malfunctions. More controversially, he concluded that these formations were not natural geological formations, but artificial structures. Most appeared around the peak of Mount Ampere, the volcano that Dr. Ewing determined had collapsed into the sea within the past 10,000 years.

Although the base of Mount Ampere plummets more than 9,842 ft (3,000 m), its plateau-like summit is a mere 213 ft (65 m) beneath the ocean surface. It was here that Russian scientists found most of the features that appeared to them human-made. These included a wall 30 in (75 cm) wide, 5 ft (1.5 m) high and slightly longer in length. Other "masonry" consisted of five broad steps

This map shows the ocean floor in the Atlantic. Off the coast of Portugal can be seen a ring of mountains matching Plato's description of Atlantis.

be only a fraction of the city's uppermost portions. This constant deposition of silt, which has gradually but continuously descended over the ruins for millennia, will make their detection difficult in the extreme.

Would Any Remains Have Survived the Cataclysm?

Even if, through technological advances, it becomes possible one day to investigate what lies beneath the silt, Atlantologists concede that the chance of finding ruins of any kind down there are fairly low. Any cataclysm, they suggest, powerful enough to have sunk an entire island the size of the Horseshoe Seamounts, or even the much smaller dimensions of Mount Ampere, "in a single day and a night," would probably have left very little in the way of cultural evidence.

ascending to an expansive platform connected to another monumental staircase.

Atlantologists point out that, after such a length of time under water, any ruins would be covered by an immense mantle of silt perhaps 98 ft (30 m) or more thick. Therefore, they suggest, the structures shown in Marakuev's photographs are likely to

THE SEARCH FOR LEMURIA

In 1985, a Japanese scuba instructor was diving in the waters off Yonaguni, among the Ryukyu chain of islands. As he glided through the depths some 43 ft (13 m) beneath the clear, blue Pacific, the diver was suddenly confronted by what appeared to be a great stone building heavily encrusted with coral.

Yonaguni's Drowned Enigma

Coming closer, he observed that the colossal structure was an arrangement of monolithic blocks. After circling the formation several times and photographing it with his underwater camera, he rose to the surface, reoriented himself and kicked to shore. Next day, the photographs he took appeared in Japan's leading newspapers.

The structure sparked controversy and drew crowds of diving archaeologists, media people and curious amateurs, none of whom was able to ascertain its identity. They could not even agree if it was human-made, let alone ancient or modern. Was it the remnant of some forgotten coastal defense installation from the war, or could it be something entirely different and far older? Already there were whispers of the lost culture of Mu, preserved in legend as the vanished motherland of humankind,

This artist's rendering shows the sunken monument lying in the waters off the Japanese island of Yonaguni.

which subsided beneath the waves long before the beginning of recorded time. Sceptics did not believe it was human-made at all, but an entirely natural formation. It was hard to prove one way or the other, as the enigma was sealed within a thick encrustation of coral.

Arch or Gateway?

Then, in late summer of the following year, another diver exploring the waters around Yonaguni was shocked to behold what seemed to be a massive arch or gateway of huge stone blocks. The rocks seemed well fitted together in a manner compared by some to

prehistoric masonry found among Inca cities on the other side of the Pacific. In this case, thanks to the swift currents in the area, coral had been unable to gain any foothold on the structure, leaving it unobscured in the 98-ft (30-m) visibility of the crystal-clear waters. Many were convinced it was human-made and extremely old.

Could this arch or gateway be evidence of a lost culture? Many Lemuria-seekers think so. They point out that the ancient city of Tiahuanaco in the Bolivian Andes, for example, contains two ceremonial gates. Sacred gates also appear on the Polynesian island of Tonga and on Japan.

LOST WORLD FILES

WARTIME INVESTIGATION

Forty years before the discoveries off Yonaguni, during the Second World War, U.S. Navy divers made an intriguing find in the same area. In the course of their extensive preparations to invade the island of Okinawa (the largest of the Ryuku Islands) in 1945, U.S. Navy planners issued detailed maps to the commanders of their landing craft, showing the optimum areas for quickly and safely disembarking their troops. During the invasion, several warships approached the coast to provide support for the landing craft and engage enemy shore batteries. Instead of the open water they expected to find, they scraped their keels along underwater obstructions not included on the maps provided by the navy planners.

After the battle, divers went over the side to investigate. The so-called "hard-hat divers," who wore copper helmets pumped with air supplied by their shipmates above, expected to find a secret enemy installation. Instead, they were surprised to see what appeared to be a massive stone platform with broad steps. The divers' brief report, made around the time of the Japanese surrender, did not describe the discovery as a modern structure. They said it appeared to be the remains of an ancient stone building. Their report may still repose somewhere in the U.S. military archives, but whatever impact it might have made at the time was utterly eclipsed by the Allies' euphoria on VJ Day.

Underwater City?

This discovery of the arch was only the first of that summer's undersea revelations. Fired by the possibility of more sunken monuments in the area, teams of expert divers fanned out from the south coast of Okinawa using standard grid-search patterns. Before the onset of autumn, they found, near three Japanese islands, five more sub-surface sites that contained what appeared to them human-made structures. The locations of these sites vary from depths of 98 ft (30 m) to 20 ft (6 m), but to their discoverers, they all seem human-made and even stylistically linked.

The sites were said to comprise paved streets and crossroads, huge altar-like formations, grand staircases leading to broad plazas and processional ways surmounted by pairs of towering features resembling pylons. The sunken structures cover the ocean bottom (although not continuously) from the small island of Yonaguni in the southwest, to Okinawa and its neighboring islands, Kerama and Aguni – comprising some 313 miles (500 km) of underwater terrain. Researchers speculate that further exploration may reveal more structures linking Yonaguni with Okinawa, and these individual sites may prove to be separate components of a large sunken island lying at the bottom of the Pacific.

Seeker's Account

WHAT DO SCIENTISTS SAY ABOUT THE YONAGUNI FORMATION?

Some of those who have studied the formation, such as geologist Robert Schoch of Boston University and archaeologist John Anthony West, state that it is most likely a natural formation, possibly used and modified by humans in the past. Schoch observes that the sandstones that make up the Yonaguni formation "are ... criss-crossed by numerous sets of parallel and vertical ... joints and fractures. Yonaguni lies in an earthquake-prone region; such earthquakes tend to fracture the rocks in a regular manner." He also observes that on the northeast coast of Yonaguni there are regular formations similar to those seen at the so-called "monument." Patrick D. Nunn, professor of oceanic geoscience at the University of the South Pacific, has studied the structures extensively and notes that the structures below the water continue above and are slate that "has been fashioned solely by natural processes" and "there seems no reason to suppose that they are artificial." Other examples of natural formations with flat faces and sharp straight edges are the basalt columns of the Giant's Causeway and the natural staircase formation on Old Rag Mountain.

The largest of these mysterious structures so far discovered lies near the eastern shore of Yonaguni, 98 ft (30 m) down. It is approximately 243 ft (74 m) long, 98 ft (30 m) across and 46 ft (14 m) high. Like the other structures, it is made

Giant's Causeway is an example of naturally occurring structures that appear to be human-made. Might this be the explanation for the underwater "ruins" found near Yonaguni?

of granitic sandstone. So far, no internal passages or chambers have been found in any of these structures.

Comparisons to Land Structures

Some Lemuria-seekers compare the undersea structures to ancient buildings on Okinawa, such as Nakagusuku Castle, and burial vaults near Noro where the islanders' ancestors are interred. The Okinawan term for these vaults is *moai*, the same word used by Polynesians of Easter Island, 6,036 miles (9,657 km) away, to describe the large-headed statues dedicated to their ancestors. Lemuria-seekers see this as more than mere coincidence, but evidence of a single, long-vanished ocean-spanning culture.

They have even claimed to find resemblances between the Yonaguni structures and *heiau* found in the distant Hawaiian Islands. *Heiau* are temples of long stone ramparts leading to great staircases surmounted by broad plazas, where wooden shrines and carved idols were placed. Lemuria-seekers concede that the Yonaguni examples differ structurally, as they comprise enormous single blocks, while the *heiau* are made up of far more numerous, smaller stones.

Spiral Staircase

In the spring of 1998, divers encountered another mysterious formation 703 miles (1,125 km) from Okinawa. The find is located near the uninhabited islet of Okinoshima in the Korean Strait, 28 miles (45 km) off the mainland at Kyushu.

One of the divers, Shun-Ichiroh Moriyama, observed what appeared to be a row of huge pillars standing

Seeker's Account

DESCRIBING OKINOSHIMA

Professor Nobuhiro Yoshida, president of the Japan Petroglyph Society, made the following observations about the so-called "spiral staircase" of Okinoshima:

"Comparing these linear steps, so perfectly suited to anyone climbing them, with the immediate subsurface environment, we notice at once that the sea bottom is otherwise composed exclusively of irregular, round boulders … and therefore in sharp contrast to the vertical columns and rising staircase."

The underwater blocks appeared to be a staircase curling around the outside of a tower.

more than 98 ft (30 m) beneath the surface, about 1,312 ft (400 m) off the northeastern shore of Okinoshima. He counted four of them, each one an enormous 23 to 33 ft (7 to 10 m) across and almost 98 ft (30 m) tall. On closer inspection, divers realized that they resembled not pillars but round stone towers, one of which appeared to have a spiral staircase winding around its exterior. For some, this tower called to mind an Australian Aboriginal folk tale of a drowned "Land of Perfection," with a great "crystal cone" tower entwined with a spiralling "snake."

News of this discovery made the front pages of Japan's major newspapers, and prompted the making of a television documentary about the find, including underwater video coverage of the peculiar structures. Even in the clear waters of the Korean Strait they were not easily photographed, however, owing to their great size. Subsurface visibility of more than 98 ft (30 m) is needed to see the monuments in their entirety, but around Okinosha, visibility extends no further than 43 to 52 ft (13 to 16 m). But the grand "staircase" spiralling around the tower farthest to the east was photographed. Divers from the university at Fukuoka measured its steps and found them to be uniformly cut to a depth of 16 in (40 cm), with a width varying from 59 to 71 in (150 to 180 cm).

Oceanographic Research

Despite an abundance of Pacific islander folk traditions describing a sunken homeland, the first accurate sonar-generated maps of the ocean bottom reveal nothing resembling a lost continent. The charts do nonetheless show areas of the Pacific that were dry land until relatively recently.

The Archipel des Tuamotu is a large collection of shallow features running northwest to southeast about 21 miles (33 km) northeast of Tahiti. Other formerly above-water areas include the Emperor Seamount Chain, extending from north to south in the western Pacific, the Caroline Seamounts and the Shatsky Rise. Taken together, these suggest a prehistoric Pacific containing rather more dry land than was previously imagined.

The chart also shows a sometimes very shallow and long, relatively thin ridge of subsurface islands running in a chain from the southern tip of Japan and connected to Taiwan, including the Ryukyu chain, where the sunken monuments were found at Okinawa, Yonaguni and other islands. Lemuria-seekers concede that this is not evidence of a sunken continent. Nonetheless, they contend, these once-dry lands comprised large territories over which a Lemurian civilization may once have spread across part of the Pacific Ocean.

OTHER LOST WORLDS

Atlantis and Lemuria may be humankind's most famous lost civilizations, but there are other phantom realms that play powerful roles in the mythology of different peoples. The lure of these fabled worlds, and the riches they may contain, have tempted many explorers to try and find them.

The Seven Cities of Gold

Invading Spaniards in the early 16th century observed Colombia's Chibchan Indians practicing the so-called Guatavita ceremony in commemoration of their forefather, a legendary golden king. The Spanish convinced themselves the king's city, "El Dorado," still existed somewhere in the Colombian interior, and they spent several fruitless centuries searching for it.

While the conquistadors were searching for El Dorado across Colombia, their comrades in North America marched after the legendary Seven Cities of Gold. The cities were sometimes collectively referred to as Quivira or Cíbola, and their story predated the Spanish Conquest by 350 years. It began in 1150 CE, when seven bishops and their congregations fled Spain by ship, carrying away certain religious relics, before the Moors could seize the city of Mérida.

The refugees were never heard from again, and it was rumored that they had crossed the Atlantic Ocean to land on another continent,

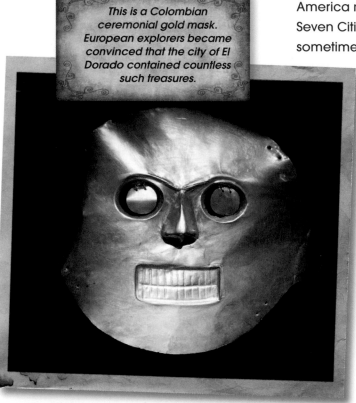

This is a Colombian ceremonial gold mask. European explorers became convinced that the city of El Dorado contained countless such treasures.

where they set up seven cities, one for each bishop, soon growing rich in gold and precious stones. The legend persisted over the centuries, but its popularity swelled following the Spanish conquest of Mexico.

Place of the Seven Caves

In 1519, the Aztec emperor Moctezuma II told the leader of the Spanish conquistadors, Hernán Cortés, that the Aztecs had previously lived to the north of their current capital, Tenochtitlan, in a place called Chicomoztoc. Hearing its translation as the "Place of the Seven Caves," the Spanish concluded that the Aztecs' former residence was none other than the fabled Cíbola. In reality, Chicomoztoc was either Rock Lake in distant Wisconsin or a large if humble settlement built around a height near the present-day town of San Isidro Culhuacan, 63 miles (100 km) northeast of the Valley of Mexico. Neither place contained any gold.

Spurred on by inflated claims for Chicomoztoc and other local tales describing far-off cities overflowing with riches, Viceroy Antonio de Mendoza dispatched an expedition led by Marcos de Niza, a Franciscan monk, in search of Cíbola. After ten months, de Niza returned to claim that he had visited a populous urban center whose residents ate from dishes of gold and silver, decorated their houses with turquoise and adorned themselves

with enormous pearls, emeralds and other stunning gems. Certain that the Seven Cities of Gold were there for the taking, de Mendoza ordered their conquest. The expedition was led by Francisco Vásquez de Coronado, who set out from Culiacán at the head of the viceroy's well-equipped army on April 22, 1540. But by the time he reached the Arizona desert, Coronado realized that de Niza had lied.

LEGENDARY TALES

MOUNTAIN RANGE OF SILVER

In South America, Spanish invaders were lured into the interior with hopes of finding Sierra de la Plata, the "Mountain Range of Silver." Survivors of an early-16th-century shipwreck on the Argentine coast had received abundant gifts of silver from the natives, who spoke of several mountains rich in the metal. Soon afterward the Spaniards discovered the estuary of the Uruguay and Paraná Rivers, which they called the Río de la Plata, the "River of Silver," known in English as the Plate River, because they believed it led to Sierra del Plata. Although the Río de la Plata became a prosperous mining area, the Mountain Range of Silver was never found. Nevertheless, as a demonstration of the power of myth, Argentina derived its name from the Latin word for "silver," *argentum.*

City of the Caesars

A myth arose that ancient Roman sailors, fleeing civil unrest following Julius Caesar's assassination, were shipwrecked on the Straits of Magellan at the southern tip of South America. For many decades following the discovery of the New World, rumors spread of El Ciudad de los Césares, the "City of the Caesars," also known as the "City of the Patagonia." The city was said to be awash with gold, silver and diamonds given by grateful Incas in gratitude for Roman help in building them an extensive network of roads.

The City of the Caesars was never found, but some intriguing discoveries have been made that suggest the Romans may well have reached South America. For example, a Roman shipwreck was investigated by underwater archaeologist Robert Marx, off Rio de Janeiro, in 1976. Amphorae he retrieved from the vessel were analyzed by Elizabeth Will, a professor in Classical Greek history at the University of Massachusetts. She positively identified them as part of a cargo from the Mediterranean port of Zilis, dating to around 250 CE. Marx went on to find a bronze fibula – a garment clasp – in Brazil's Guanabarra Bay.

Farther north, near the Mexican Gulf Coast, bricks used to build the Mayan city of Comalcalco were found to be stamped with second-century CE Roman

Seeker's Account

ROMAN INFLUENCE IN SOUTH AMERICA?

According to American archaeologist Gunnar Thompson, an Inca aqueduct at Rodadero, Peru, "employs two tiers of rounded, stone arches often referred to as "true arches." This style of architecture was a characteristic of the ancient Mediterranean. Consequently, the Rodadero aqueduct makes a strong argument for Greco-Roman cultural diffusion."

mason marks, while its terracotta plumbing – unique in all Mesoamerica – was identical to contemporary pipes found in Israel. These and similar finds – such as the ceramic representation of a bearded European with a Roman-style haircut and wearing a typically Roman cap, retrieved during the excavation of a second-century CE pyramid at Caliztlahuaca, Mexico – suggest that the legend of the "City of the Caesars" may have some basis in truth.

Antilia

Antilia is a legendary island that was reputed to lie in the Atlantic Ocean, far to the west of Portugal and Spain. The earliest known description of Antilia appeared in a biography of the Roman military commander Quintus Sertorius, written by the historian Plutarch in 74

The City of the Caesars was, according to legend, a place of extraordinary wealth, resplendent with Inca treasures.

CE. According to Plutarch, in about 83 BCE, during Sertorius's consulship in Spain, he "met some sailors who had recently come back from the Atlantic islands, two in number separated by a very narrow strait and lie 10,000 furlongs from Africa." The sailors described Antilia as a utopian realm with fertile soil and a fine climate, producing plenty of food for its happy people.

Antilia was more or less forgotten until the 15th century when voyages of discovery into the Atlantic Ocean rekindled interest in the island. In a Portuguese version of the Spanish Cíbola myth, it was said that seven Portuguese bishops and their parishioners rediscovered Antilia after fleeing from the Moorish conquest of Iberia. After their arrival on the island, they supposedly founded the cities of Aira, Anhuib, Ansalli, Ansesseli, Ansodi, Ansolli and Con. Nuremberg geographer Martin Behaim repeated the legend on his 1492 globe of the Earth. An inscription on the globe stated that the crew of a Spanish vessel sighted Antilia in 1414 and Portuguese sailors landed there during the 1430s. Antilia had been included in European maps from as early as 1424, and the renowned mathematician Paul Toscanelli advised Christopher Columbus before his 1492 voyage that Antilia was the principal landmark for measuring the distance between Lisbon and Zipangu (Japan).

The island of Antilia was usually depicted as an almost perfect rectangle, its long axis running north–south, but with seven or eight bays between the east and west coasts. This shape bears a vague resemblance to Puerto Rico, which led some geographers to believe that Puerto Rico was indeed Plutarch's Antilia. As a consequence, the Caribbean islands became known as the Antilles.

Antilia in the Azores?

Antilia has also been identified by some as San Miguel, the largest island in the Azores. San Miguel matches Plutarch's description in terms of distance from Morocco – 1,141 miles (1,825 km) – but its shape and size does not match its representation on Renaissance maps. Antilia was usually shown about the size of Portugal, which is 35,645 sq miles (92,090 sq km), but San Miguel is just 287 sq miles (744.5 sq km).
The Azores were uninhabited at the time of their discovery in 1427, but the the Portugese sailors who first landed

there found evidence of previous visitors from Europe. Inside a cave on Santa Maria, the Portuguese stumbled upon a stone altar adorned with serpentine designs. At Corvo, a small

Could San Miguel in the Azores be the real Antilia?

LOST WORLD FILES

THE DRAGON'S ISLE

Fifteenth-century Arab geographers referred to Antilia as Jezirat al Tennyn, the "Dragon's Isle," evoking an island of active volcanoes, a description that hardly fits Puerto Rico. San Miguel, however, boasts numerous volcanoes, one of which, interestingly, is known as Sete Cidades, the "Seven Cities." Its caldera is about 53 miles (5 km) across, with walls some 1,640 ft (500 m) high. Sete Cidades has erupted at least eight times since 1444; another of the island's volcanoes, Agua de Pau, erupted for almost a month in 1563; an unnamed group of volcanoes erupted in 1652; and, just offshore, the Monaco Bank submarine volcano blew up in 1907, and again four years later. But San Miguel's largest, most dangerous volcano is Furnas. With a summit caldera about 3.75 miles (6 km) in diameter and 984 to 1,312 ft (300 to 400 m) deep, Furnas generated a week-long eruption in 1630, which claimed the lives of more than 200 people, mostly in swift, boiling mud flows. With this record, San Miguel certainly matches Arabic descriptions of Antilia as the "Dragon's Isle."

cask of Phoenician coins dating to the fifth century BCE was found.

A more dramatic find was a bronze equestrian statue on top of a mountain on San Miguel itself. It was 16 ft (5 m) tall with a stone pedestal bearing a badly weathered inscription. On top of a magnificently crafted horse sat the rider with his right arm stretched forward to point across the sea toward the west. When notified of the discovery, King John V ordered it removed to Portugal, but the statue slipped from its improvised halter and crashed down the side of the mountain. The rider's head, one arm and the horse's head and flank alone survived the fall. These fragments, together with an impression of the pedestal's inscription, were sent to the king.

They were preserved in his royal palace in Lisbon, where scholars were baffled by what they described as the inscription's "archaic Latin." They could only decipher one word from it – *cates* – but its meaning eluded them. Atlantologists point out that the word is close to *cati*, which means "go that way" in Quechua, the language spoken by the Incas. Unfortunately, modern scholars have been denied the chance of further investigation of the statue and inscription: in 1755, all the artifacts removed from San Miguel were lost during the great earthquake that destroyed most of Lisbon.

Antilia's mysterious allure persists into the 21st century. In 2007, Canadian architect and amateur archaeologist Paul Chiasson published his controversial book *Island of Seven Cities*, in which he identified the island of Cape Breton, south of Newfoundland, with Antilia. Stone structures of unknown origin, and oral traditions among the local Micmac Indians of seafaring foreigners, led him to conclude that Chinese sailors, some of them Nestorian Christians, rounded Africa and sailed up the Atlantic before Cape Breton was officially discovered by John Cabot in 1497.

Hyperborea

The icy northern regions of the Earth have always exerted a fascination on people, both ancient and modern, and they have often been the subject of rumor and myth. In Greek mythology, Hyperborea, meaning "Beyond the North Wind," was a mythical land existing far to the north. In this perfect place, the Greeks said, the sun shines for 24 hours a day, every day of the year, except one, when the sun rises and sets just once. In this they were not far from the truth, for beyond the Arctic Circle the sun does shine for 24 hours a day – for half the year, at least, between the vernal and autumnal equinoxes. This has persuaded some scholars to conclude that the ancient Greeks visited the Arctic Circle.

There is other evidence to support the idea that the Greeks reached the Arctic:

The great temple of Hyperborea supposedly resembled Stonehenge, the prehistoric monument near Salisbury, England.

their hero Heracles sought the golden-antlered hind in Hyperborea. It turns out that the Arctic-dwelling reindeer is the only deer species in which the female bears horns.

The poet Pindar (552–443 BCE) said the Hyperboreans lived long lives "far from labor and battle." They were a pious people who devoted all their time to the worship of a single deity – Apollo, god of the sun, who allegedly spent his winters among them. Each year, on Apollo's feast day, a Greek religious sect, the Hyperborean maidens, carried mysterious gifts packed in straw to the sun god's temple at Delos, his birthplace in the Aegean Sea. The bleached ruins of the Temple of the Hyperborean Maidens on Delos can be visited to this day.

Yet a cult dedicated to the worship of the sun god would seem a little unlikely in the Arctic. Other ancient writers, such as Hecataeus of Abdera and the Roman historian and geographer Strabo, placed Hyperborea in Britain. Indeed, some modern researchers have compared their description of the Hyperboreans' main temple to Stonehenge, Britain's most famous megalithic monument. Stonehenge may well have been used for sun worship because its design allows for the prediction of eclipse, solstice, equinox and other celestial events. By the time Hecataeus wrote *On the Hyperboreans* in the fourth century

BCE, the builders of Stonehenge had long since vanished, and their site had been taken over by Druid priests. It would have been the druids that contemporaries of Hecataeus would have observed, if they had visited Stonehenge.

Thule

Another mysterious Arctic realm is Thule. This legendary land was supposedly visited by the ancient Greek merchant, geographer and explorer Pytheas in the fourth century BCE. In his book *On the Ocean*, Pytheas narrates the story of his decade-long travels beyond the Mediterranean Sea, beginning in 330 BCE. He records that Thule is a six-day sail north of Britain and is near the "frozen sea."

Seeker's Account

LONG DAYS AND NIGHTS

Pliny the Elder's *Natural History* described Thule:

"… in which there be no nights at all, as we have declared, about mid-summer, namely when the Sun passes through the sign Cancer; and contrariwise no days in mid-winter: and each of these times they suppose, do last six months, all day, or all night."

Thule was associated by the ancient Greeks with the aurora borealis, the Northern Lights.

Pytheas had been sent on a fact-finding mission by the Greek colony of Massalia (today's Marseille, France) to learn more about certain trade goods, particularly tin and amber. Some Atlantologists believe he may also have had an unofficial reason for embarking on the voyage: Plato had written of Atlantis just 20 years earlier, and perhaps Pytheas was hoping to find remnants of the legendary island.

Pytheas' alleged route took him from Massalia through the Straits of Gibraltar to Bordeaux, Nantes, Land's End, Plymouth, the Isle of Man, the Outer Hebrides, Orkney, Britain's east coast, Kent, Heligoland and (possibly) Iceland. In Cornwall, he studied the production and processing of tin, then sailed around Great Britain, calculating its circumference to within 2.5 percent of modern estimates. Next, so he claimed, he voyaged to Thule.

Some historians place Thule among the Orkney Islands or in Norway. However, these are unlikely settings for a mythical land as first-millennium BCE fishermen routinely travelled between northern Great Britain, the Orkneys and the Norwegian coast. The Roman author Orosius (384–420 CE) and the early ninth-century CE Irish monk Dicuil both place Thule north and west of Ireland and Britain. Dicuil stated that it lay beyond the Faroes, which suggests that Thule may have been Iceland. In his *Against Rufinias*, the fifth-century CE Roman writer Claudian told of "Thule lying icebound beneath the pole-star," which appears to support this conclusion.

But if Iceland really was Thule, who were the people Pytheas recorded as living there? He described Thule as an agricultural country, where they produced honey and mixed it with grain to make a special drink. They also enjoyed fruits and dairy products, and threshed grain inside barns, contrary to southern European practice. Yet, according to the conventional histories, Iceland was not occupied until Norse settlers arrived there in the late ninth century CE, some 1,200 years after Pytheas supposedly visited the island.

LEGENDARY TALES

THE VOYAGE OF ST. BRENDAN

St. Brendan was a sixth-century CE Irish abbot and founder of Clonfert monastery and monastic school. According to legend, St. Brendan was preaching to the residents of the islands that lie off Ireland's western coast, when he and 17 of his fellow monks were blown out to sea. His vessel was a currach – a capacious, tubby boat with a wooden frame over which leather was stretched. The legend states that they voyaged to the other side of the ocean, where they landed on the shores of a new continent, the "Land of Promise," more often referred to as St. Brendan's Isle.

Three hundred years would pass before their adventure was written down in *Navigatio Santi Brendani Abulis* (*The Voyage of Saint Brendan the Abbot*). Marcos Martinez's *Planiferio de Ebstorf* (1234) mentions "the lost island discovered by St. Brendan, but nobody has found it since." In 1976, Irish explorer Tim Severin recreated St. Brendan's voyage in a currach, built using sixth-century methods and materials. Scrupulously following the details laid out in *Navigatio Santi Brendani Abatis*, Severin made landfall at Newfoundland. Some scholars regard Brendan's description of a "continental land" as evidence that the abbot's expedition reached America nearly a thousand years before Columbus.

Either Thule was some other place, or the islanders Pytheas met were remnants of what archaeologists currently refer to as the Red Paint People. These were Neolithic seafarers who sailed the polar route from Scandinavia to Labrador 6,000 years ago. Some researchers believe faint traces of the Red Paint People's cultural impact on Iceland have been found. Could at least a small colony of them have survived into the fourth century BCE? Their honey production and barns disqualify them as Inuit, who, in any case, never settled in Iceland.

Shambhala

Shambhala is a mythical kingdom in the Tibetan Buddhist tradition. It is often associated with Shangri-La, but the latter is a fictional place, invented by British author James Hilton in his 1933 novel *Lost Horizon*. "Shambhala" is a Sanskrit term meaning "place of peace and happiness." It came to be regarded as a perfect place, cut off from the rest of the world in a remote Himalayan valley surrounded by inaccessible mountains, where its enlightened inhabitants follow a pure form of Buddhism.

Shambhala has traditionally been associated with various sacred sites in or near Tibet, including the Tibetan capital, Lhasa. However, it may not be a place at all, but a state of mind. In Tibetan Buddhist philosophy, achieving enlightenment is sometimes referred to as arriving at a "perfect city."

This has not prevented people from seeking Shambhala. In the 1920s, two Russian expeditions tried and failed to find Shambhala. Some believed it to be Hunza, a thousand-year-old principality in northern Pakistan. This remote and verdant valley is frequently cut off for months at a time from the rest of the world due to snowfall in the surrounding mountains.

LOST WORLD FILES

SHANGRI-LA

In James Hilton's novel, Shangri-La was a mystical, harmonious valley located in the Kunlun Mountains. In modern usage, it has come to be used as a term for any earthly paradise – a permanently happy land, isolated from the outside world. Hilton was inspired by stories of Shambhala, which was being sought by Eastern and Western explorers at the time he wrote his novel. Shangri-La literally means "Shang (a region of Tibet) Mountain Pass."

Agartha

Others have linked Shambhala to Agartha, another mythical kingdom located underground. Agartha is a city apparently lit by its own subterranean sun and populated by 13-ft (4-m) tall people who will one day fulfill an ancient prophecy by establishing their divine leader as king of the world. It is possible that Agartha is based on Lhasa where an underground network of tunnels and chambers existed until the 1950s when the city was occupied by Chinese forces. Various writers and occultists have become interested in Agartha over the years and tried to find the entrance to this supposed world.

Numerous suggestions have been made, including Ecuador's "Cave of the Oil Birds," Kentucky's Mammoth Cave, the North Pole, the South Pole and the Great Pyramid of Giza.

Shambhala, if it truly exists, is a place of unparalleled beauty and tranquility.

GLOSSARY

a cappella Singing without instrumental accompaniment.

adobe A kind of clay used as a building material.

aeronautics The science of air travel.

Albion A poetic term for Britain or England.

amphorae (plural of amphora) Tall ancient Greek or Roman jars with two handles and a narrow neck.

ancestral Belonging to and inherited from one's ancestors.

antediluvian Belonging to a time before the biblical flood.

archaeologist A scholar of human history and prehistory through the excavation of sites and analysis of artifacts and other physical remains.

archetype An original model for something that has been imitated.

artifact An object made by a human being, typically something of cultural or historical interest.

asteroid A small rocky body orbiting the sun. A few enter the Earth's atmosphere as meteors.

Atlantologist A seeker of lost worlds, particularly Atlantis.

Bronze Age A prehistoric period that followed the Stone Age and preceded the Iron Age, when certain weapons and tools came to be made of bronze rather than stone.

caldera A large volcanic crater.

cartographer A mapmaker.

cataclysm A large-scale violent event in the natural world.

Caucasian Relating to one of the traditional divisions of humankind, covering a broad group of peoples from Europe, western Asia, parts of India and North Africa.

celestial mechanics The branch of astronomy that deals with the calculation of the motions of celestial objects such as planets.

ceremonial center A place where formal events of a religious or public nature are carried out.

climatologist A scientist who studies climate.

colossi (plural of colossus) Things of enormous size.

comet A celestial object consisting of a nucleus of ice and dust and, when near the sun, a "tail" of gas and dust particles.

concentric Describing circles or other shapes that share the same center, the larger ones surrounding the smaller.

conflagration A large-scale, destructive fire.

conquistadors The Spanish conquerors of Mexico and Peru in the 16th century.

core sample A cylindrical section that has been drilled out of a naturally occurring substance, such as sediment or rock, for purposes of scientific analysis.

deluge A flood.

dendrochronologist A scientist who dates events, such as environmental changes, by studying the patterns of annual growth rings in timber and tree trunks.

dialogue A work of literature that takes the form of a discussion between different people.

earthworks A large artificial bank of soil.

electroplate Coat an object with metal by passing an electric current through a solution containing metal ions (electrically charged atoms).

enlightenment The action or state of attaining spiritual knowledge.

equestrian Relating to horses.

equinox An equinox is the time of the year when day and night are of equal length. There are two equinoxes each year: the vernal (spring) equinox and the autumnal (autumn) equinox.

erosion The gradual wearing away of soil, rock or land by the actions of wind, water and other natural agents.

extraterrestrial Relating to something from outside the earth or its atmosphere.

frieze A broad horizontal band of sculpted or painted decoration.

geoglyph A large illustration produced on the ground.

geologist A scientist who studies the Earth's physical structure and substance, its history and the processes that act on it.

Heracles A Greek hero of superhuman strength who performed twelve immense tasks.

hieroglyphics A picture of an object representing a word, syllable or sound, as found in ancient Egyptian and other writing systems.

imperialist Describing a nation that seeks to extend its power and influence through military force and other means.

irrigated Describing an area of land that has been supplied with water by means of channels.

Jesuit A member of the Society of Jesus, a Roman Catholic order of priests founded in 1534 to do missionary work.

karmic (in Hinduism and Buddhism) The sum of a person's actions in this and previous states of existence, viewed as deciding their fate in future existences.

keystone A central stone in a structure, which locks the whole thing together.

linguist A person skilled in foreign languages.

magnetic field A region around a magnetic material or a moving electric charge within which the force of magnetism acts.

megalithic Relating to prehistoric monuments made of or containing large stones (megaliths).

megaton A unit of explosive power chiefly used for nuclear weapons, equivalent to one million tons of TNT.

Mesoamerica A region in the Americas, extending approximately from central Mexico to Belize, Guatemala, El Salvador, Honduras, Nicaragua and Costa Rica, within which a number of pre-Columbian societies flourished before the Spanish colonization of the Americas in the 16th and 17th centuries.

meteor A small body of matter from outer space that enters the Earth's atmosphere, becoming incandescent as a result of friction and appearing as a streak of light.

meteorite A meteor that survives its passage through the Earth's atmosphere so that part of it strikes the ground.

Neolithic Relating to the later part of the Stone Age.

occultist A follower of supernatural, mystical or magical beliefs and practices.

oceanographer A scientist who studies the physical and biological phenomena of the sea.

pagan Relating to beliefs other than those of the main world religions.

perjury The offense of willfully telling an untruth in a court of law after having taken an oath.

petroglyph A rock carving, especially an ancient one.

plate tectonics A theory explaining the structure of the Earth's crust and many associated phenomena as resulting from the interaction of rigid plates that move slowly over the underlying mantle.

Poseidon The Greek god of the sea, water, earthquakes and horses.

primate A mammal of the order that includes lemurs, monkeys, apes and humans.

principality A state ruled by a prince.

pumice A very light and porous volcanic rock formed when a gas-rich froth of glassy lava solidifies rapidly.

pylon A monumental gateway of an Egyptian temple, made up of two tapering towers.

sedimentation Matter deposited on the surface of the land or the bottom of a body of water.

seismic Relating to earthquakes or other vibrations of the Earth and its crust.

solstice Either of the two times in the year, the summer solstice and the winter solstice, when the sun reaches its highest or lowest point in the sky at noon, marked by the longest and shortest days.

sonar A system for the detection of objects under water and for measuring the water's depth by emitting sound pulses and detecting or measuring their return after being reflected.

subterranean Beneath the Earth's surface.

tenon A projecting piece of wood made for insertion into a mortise in another piece to make a joint.

theologian An expert in theology, the study of the nature of God and religious belief.

topographical Relating to the arrangement or accurate representation of the physical features of an area.

FURTHER INFORMATION

Atlantis (Edge Books) by Michael Martin (Capstone, 2007).

Atlantis (Mysterious Encounters) by Stuart A Kallen (Greenhaven Press, 2011).

Atlantis and Other Lost Cities (Graphic Mysteries) by David West (Book House, 2007).

Lost Civilizations (Mysteries Unwrapped) by Sharon Linnéa (Sterling, 2009).

The Mystery of Atlantis (Can Science Solve…?) by Holly Wallace (Heinemann Library, 2006).

The Mystery of Atlantis (Unsolved!) by Kathryn Walker (Crabtree, 2009).

Web Sites
Due to the changing nature of Internet links, Rosen Publishing has developed an online list of Web sites related to the subject of this book. This site is updated regularly. Please use this link to access the list:

http://www.rosenlinks.com/pfiles/atl

INDEX